The Divine Genogram

The Divine Genogram

The Cosmic Human Experience

Donna Evans Strauss

© **Copyright 2024 - All rights reserved.**

The content contained within this book may not be reproduced, duplicated or transmitted without direct written permission from the author or the publisher.

Under no circumstances will any blame or legal responsibility be held against the publisher, or author, for any damages, reparation, or monetary loss due to the information contained within this book, either directly or indirectly.

A special thank you to Kaho Koinuma (Digital Artist), Patricia Eshuk (Fine Artist), and Heather Kabat (Artist) for creating the images in this book, and to Brandon and Nashel for Writing Coaching, Editing, and Creative Direction.

Legal Notice:

This book is copyright protected. It is only for personal use. You cannot amend, distribute, sell, use, quote or paraphrase any part, or the content within this book, without the consent of the author or publisher.

Disclaimer Notice:

Please note the information contained within this document is for educational and entertainment purposes only. All effort has been executed to present accurate, up to date, reliable, complete information. No warranties of any kind are declared or implied. Readers acknowledge that the author is not engaged in the rendering of legal, financial, medical or professional advice. The content within this book has been derived from various sources. Please consult a licensed professional before attempting any techniques outlined in this book.

By reading this document, the reader agrees that under no circumstances is the author responsible for any losses, direct or indirect, that are incurred as a result of the use of the information contained within this document, including, but not limited to, errors, omissions, or inaccuracies.

Dedication

In memory of Barbara Ann Brennan, a pioneer in the field of Human Energy Consciousness Studies, a true mentor and guide for the evolution of consciousness of humanity. I am forever grateful for her leadership and belief in my spiritual journey. Thank you Beloved Teacher!

Incarnation and Transfiguration

When you first went through
the idea of man
into the physical world, you began
a great endeavor.

At this stage
Of your evolutionary endeavor,
You are walking into transfiguration.
It has taken millions of years

To reach this moment,
And yet this moment
Has always been within you.

:- Barbara Ann Brennan
Seeds Of The Spirit

Table of Contents

Introduction — 1
Discovering the Divine Genogram — 4
The Cosmic Miracle of Incarnation — 7

Inner & Outer Space: Multidimensional Paradigm — 13
The Holographic Universe
A Glimpse Beyond the 3D — 15
Foundational Ideas — 17
Development & Refinement — 18
Ongoing Research — 19
The Multiverse — 20
Quantum Entanglement — 21

The Divine Mind & the Realms of Consciousness — 27
The Universal & Divine Mind — 28
Realms of Consciousness — 31
Examples of Realms of Consciousness — 31
Akashic Records & Collective Consciousness — 34
Lower Realms as States of Consciousness — 40
Multidimensional Paradigm — 43

Human Energy Consciousness System — 47
Solid Matter vs. Energy Fields — 53
The Four Dimensions of Humankind — 55
The Hara Dimension — 59
The Human Energy Consciousness Field — 63
The Physical Dimension — 66

The Seven Stages of Incarnation — 69
Stage One: Core Star — 72
Stage Two: Hara Dimension — 74
Stage Three: Development of the Double Torus — 76
The Rats That Changed Morphogenetics — 80
Stage Four: Cell Division — 82

Stage Five: Zygote	84
Stage Six: Fetus in Utero	86
Stage Seven: The Infant	88
Epigenetics	90
Biology of Belief	91

Human Evolution: Essence Into Matter   95

James Leininger	95
Everything Is Energy	98
Chakras System: Information Transmission	99
The Case of Musaigwa	103
Centripetal & Centrifugal Forces in Chakras	106

Family System: Awakening the Divine Genogram   113

Expansion & Integration of Family Systems	115
Tele in Family Systems	116
Constellations in Family Systems	118
Therapeutic Process in Family Constellations	121
Family Biofield: The Divine Genogram	123
Family Systems & the Seven Stages of Incarnation	125
The Divine Genogram	127

How to Do a Genogram   133

Setting Up Your Genogram	136
Step 1: Gather Basic Family Information	138
Step 2: Map Out Relationships	140
Step 3: Identify Relationship Issues	141
Step 4: Recognize Family Beliefs	142
Step 5: Connect Patterns to Spiritual Insights	144
The Genogram, Trauma, & Divine Qualities	146

Trauma Perspectives   149

Trauma & the Human Biofield	152
Trauma at the Seventh Level & Seventh Chakra	155
Trauma at the Sixth Level & Sixth Chakra	158
Trauma at the Fifth Level & Fifth Chakra	160
Trauma on the Fourth Level & Fourth Chakra	162
Trauma on the Third (Mental) Level	166
Trauma on the Second (Emotional) Level	169

Trauma on the First (Physical) Level   170

Unveiling Divine Qualities   **175**

Practice the I AM Meditation for Healing   176
The Seven Innate Divine Qualities   186
Divine Trust   188
Divine Self-Love & Self-Acceptance   190
Divine Respect   191
Divine Relational Love   192
Divine Communication   193
Divine Vision   195
Divine Wisdom   196
Example From CB   196
Forgiveness Heals Generational Trauma   199

Collective Awakening   **203**

Transformation in Your Personal Life   204
Transformation in Your Work & Business   205
Community & World Transformation   206
Embark on Your Journey   207

Glossary   **211**

References   **218**

PART 1

Introduction

Have you ever had a voice inside nudging you to explore an idea, topic, or thought you were not currently interested in? This is what happened to me from 2002 to 2011. At the time, I was teaching at The Barbara Brennan School, and I continued to hear this voice citing different biblical passages in my spirit through this time. I found this quite confusing since I had not attended church since I was in the 6th grade. Rather, my childhood years were riddled with family challenges, changing schools, and moving from town to town. Yet, I knew that voice. I had heard it before, nudging me to explore a path less taken by my friends or classmates. I remembered it from when I was studying Mental Health Technology at Hahnemann University Medical School in Philadelphia. This same voice was present to inspire my growth and search for knowledge and truth.

Then, my main interest was how consciousness is transmitted from one person to another. I had several experiences as a child and into adulthood where this phenomenon happened to me. I would have other thoughts and feelings that I knew were not my own and this was confusing yet compelled me to search for answers. One evening after kissing my husband good night, my mind wandered again to these very questions. How does consciousness transmit knowledge from one person to the next? I wondered if there was a school that taught about this phenomenon. If so, I would love to study and attend. Only a few weeks later, a gentleman I did not know at the time, Tad McKeon, handed me *Hands of Light: A Guide to Healing through the Human Energy Field.* Brennan had self-published her book, and McKeon was one of her clients.

When I opened the book my life changed, the answers I was searching for were there in black and white. In 1987 I entered her four-year training program and by 1994 I became the Department Head of Healing Science. From 2000-2005, I became the Dean of Year 4 studies, and during the same time I was developing and teaching a master's level supervision training program for healers. After 24 years, the program is still running as the Advanced Studies Brennan Integration Work. So, you can see how a nudge, prodding me to read the Bible felt like a detour from the path I was on. Yet, the voice was strong. I would hear statements like, Donna, everything you are teaching here is within the understanding of this one passage. After a few years of hearing this voice, I decided to retire from teaching and explore where the voice was leading me. The nudging led me to dive contemplatively into reading the Bible from the beginning to the end. I was a novice and had so much resistance.

The path led me to unfold my family history, to unearth secrets from the past, and heal generations of pain. Through the knowledge of the research, I was led to create *Blessings From a Thousand Generations,* which offered me a guide into the unknown and opened sacred knowledge that I was so strongly inclined to discard as myth. I felt like a novice, unprepared and resistant to the words on the page. Yet, I committed to reading and debating with the still small voice inside. I finally surrendered and wrote the book.

For this book, *The Divine Genogram: The Cosmic Human Experience,* I was nudged again to revisit *Blessings from a Thousand Generations* and understand the gems that are still in it to be explored. The paradigm shift in physics, cosmology, and archeology, opened pathways and insights to the information I received when I wrote Blessings. At the time, I was resistant and fearful to write down some of my experiences, even while contemplating and meditating on the first chapter. Some of the insights seemed improbable at the time, and that I should leave well enough alone. I can share now one of my struggles with reading Genesis was the story of Adam's Rib. "Oh boy," I said, "you must think I am naive to believe that people are born from a rib". Like I mentioned before, I could not read any further. This is where my logical mind could not bend. I left the book and refused to read further until one night at 2 AM. That voice woke me again and asked me to go downstairs and turn on my computer. I said, "Okay, it is 2 AM, you know!" I turned on my computer, and the voice said, "Look up a ribcage." "Okay, I said, here is a ribcage, so?" The voice answered, "Now pull up a DNA strand." "Okay, here is a DNA strand." It was showing the spiral of a double helix. Again, the voice says, "Scroll down." "Okay, I said." I scrolled down and saw the unfolded DNA Strand then put the image side by side with the rib cage. The voice again said, "XX and XY". I was confused at first, then something deep inside knew that perhaps there was more to the story of incarnation than I was led to believe. Humbly, I decided to read the next paragraph and let myself take in this new information. I took a risk and shared my experience a few times with people close to me. It all sounds crazy, I know, and it goes way beyond the current knowledge base.

In *The Divine Genogram*, I am ready to explore and share with you, the seven stages of incarnation and my contemplative understanding of our journey as cosmic beings of light. This is my interpretation and theory of how we enter the earth plane and interpenetrate the morphogenetic biofield surrounding the earth. I do not have any answers to the origins of our species. Rather, I am continually inquiring into what I now believe is the "Library of Congress" or "Hall of Records," stored within the DNA and the infinite intelligent field that interpenetrates and connects all of us. Like bits of information stored within different programs on a computer, the DNA strands are turned on by the electromagnetic field provided by the core light expressed through the different dimensions of our being. In *Blessings*, I refer to the family genogram, from family systems theory as the God Realization Genogram and introduce the concept of God being the foundation of all life. Here in *The Divine Genogram*, I continue to believe that God, the Infinite Intelligent Universe, is the fabric from which we emerge and attempt to interweave current physics, spirituality, energy healing theories, family systems, and neuropsychology to explore a simplistic path toward a holistic way to healing trauma.

Discovering the Divine Genogram

When I started learning about consciousness, I had no idea I would end up here. Such is the nature of journeys like this one—as you learn and experience the power of knowledge, you do not know how impactful it will be on you and the people you meet along the way. I am so humbled that I am here, however, and I recognize that this book and the information it contains are milestones in my life's purpose.

In *Blessings From a Thousand Generations*, I shared how Moses' life and mine have similar beginnings. We both started in adoptive families and had to find who we were before we could discover our purpose and destiny. In the same way, we both also stood against the negative love bonds that were within our families—his being slavery—and we found a way to bring freedom in instead.

There is one more resemblance that I have realized, and it helps me understand the work I am doing now. In Exodus 24–34:18 (*Holy Bible, New International Version,* 2013/1973), we find Moses going up Mount Sinai, an act of ascension to a higher plane. We know that his ascension to Mount Sinai was not only physical because while he was there, but he also interacted intimately with the infinite universe. One concept we will explore in this book is how the crown chakra leads to the astral plane. The crown chakra is a vortex that allows the soul to move between the world above—the astral plane or Heaven—and this natural world we live in. So, Moses' body went up the mountain, but his soul also ascended to a higher form of consciousness where he met with God.

What's even more interesting is that when he came down, his face was shining. We know from the human energy consciousness system (HECS) that the glow on the face of Moses was the reflection of the light and energy within him, which he had unlocked during his time on the mountain. Just as Moses was on the mountain for 40 days and nights, Jesus spent the same amount of time in the desert praying and fasting before he went out to start his ministry.

In the same way, I have spent time improving my understanding of the human energy field and improving my knowledge of the topic overall. To be exact, I have 40 years of experience in the field of consciousness studies. I have not always understood the things I do now, but I have taken the time to learn many different concepts from many other experts—of whom Barbara Ann Brennan has had the most impact. My journey has been intertwined with education, experience, practice, and teaching thousands of students from around the world.

Throughout my journey, I have wanted to help people understand who they are and how to use that information to bring holistic healing to their lives. In my first book, *Blessings From a Thousand Generations*: What Our Biblical Ancestors Can Teach Us Today, I explore how our biblical ancestors—mine being Moses—could unlock the keys to our personal, familial, and societal healing.

My family had its share of problems and haunting hidden secrets. I did not know any of my relatives other than my father. My family tree was withered, with all the leaves falling off—except for the branch that had my father and two brothers. I later learned that my father was not my biological parent, but his dad adopted me—just like Pharaoh's house did Moses. There were no mothers in my life, from either the paternal or the maternal side. I could have been one of those missing children posted on the side of a milk carton.

These events early in my childhood sparked a curiosity for self-discovery that set me on a path to uncover my roots. First, I met my estranged mother, who was thought to be deceased, and she helped me shed light on what had happened to my family tree. I am grateful for this path, though; it has brought me fulfillment and spilled over the healing to so many others.

In the late 1980s, I entered the mental health program at

Hahnemann University in Philadelphia and interned at Horsham Clinic in Horsham, PA. This period in my life was invaluable because it allowed me to combine my love for people with the chance to work with those who needed restoration. Around the same time, the field of psychology was moving from a Freudian-based model to a more humanistic mode, a move that remains one of the most important in the history of psychology.

I remember how child guidance and family systems theories emerged around that time, and my soul was interested in them. I delved into as many psychological modalities that gave insight into human consciousness and health. Dr Hugh Rosen, the Department Head of Mental Health Technology at Hahnemann University and co-author of Constructing Realities: Meaning-Making Perspectives for Psychologists, supported my inquiry into the work of Barbara Ann Brennan. Both programs challenged my way of comparing psychological modalities with a scientific inquiry into human energy consciousness studies.

I dove into family systems work, and as part of it, I had to create my family genogram. That was when it hit me: There weren't any relatives on the tree except for my stepmother's family. This realization propelled me to delve even deeper and understand who I was and gave me the desire to help others do the same.

While studying at Hahnemann, I was also intrigued by consciousness studies. I had a clairvoyant mind from a very young age, but at that point, I did not know I was being drawn toward my divine assignment. I can remember knowing things about other people or situations beyond what anyone in my family would discuss. It was almost as if my mind was connected to another bandwidth and could pick out information that no one else could. I wanted to understand this phenomenon better. I knew I wasn't psychic, nor did I have any special gifts, yet I didn't have a language for the type of phenomenon I was experiencing.

I would ask people questions and share my experiences to see if anyone else was like that, but there were no real answers. There were several instances where I prayed, and then something would happen immediately after—like the one time a pastor arrived at the juvenile center I was working at in 1978 to confirm what I had been praying about. I share this story in more detail in *Blessings From a Thousand Generations*. Another time, I prayed, and it helped me find my mother—and the phenomena continued.

My friends would always tell me not to worry about it, but I couldn't do so; I needed answers. It wasn't until I met my husband Jeff that things got better. He noticed and pointed out that when I said something, it would often come true—more often than coincidence would be able to explain. Jeff encouraged my exploration, until one night I prayed that I wanted to learn about these phenomena and how people heal. Within a week, I was handed Barbara Ann Brennan's self-published book *Hands of Light: A Guide Through the Human Energy Field*. In 1987, I decided to enter her program alongside my studies at Hahnemann. This decision changed my life, and I found a family at the school. I became the Department Head of Healing Science in 1994 and served in that post until 2000, when I became the Dean of Fourth-Year Studies. At the same time, I became the designer and professor of what is now called the Advanced Studies Brennan Integration Program, which was—at inception—my Project Demonstrating Excellence for Union Institute.

In the culmination of these years of work, I have modified my theories on the God-realization genogram, which were presented in my first edition of *Blessings From a Thousand Generations*, into the divine genogram. I have now expanded on these theories and observations to include our religious and spiritual heritages, quantum physics, Sacred Geometry, neuropsychology, advanced insights into the HECS, and incarnation. I have come to understand that we are cosmic beings who have traveled here to advance human evolution.

The Cosmic Miracle of Incarnation

In The Divine Genogram, we expand on the ideas in *Blessings From a Thousand Generations* to help you fully understand your origin. While we are born of our mothers and fathers through a biological phenomenon, there is a miracle far greater than that at play. The miracle of your creation will point to your true origin: the divine universe itself.

You are a beam of light that has existed outside of this reality for eternity but chose to incarnate in this world in this season. In the same way that light burst from a single point to spawn the universe as we know it, you also had a beginning just as cosmic and miraculous. Your mother's womb resembles the dark and void space that the spirit of God hovered over before the light of the world sprung into existence. Your light burst through from that dark and void space, creating life as you know it. This act transcended time and space, bringing your light from another realm into this reality. In that moment of appointment, your essence was tethered to the DNA of your mother and your father; the cosmic light that once existed out of space and time found its place within space and time. The miracle that started there continued as cells divided and multiplied, the cosmic explosion of creation taking place as you began your journey as a human being.

The Divine Genogram is your pathway to understanding this supernatural inheritance. You are more than your physical body, and your life is more than the experiences you have gathered during your days here. Rather, your beginning is tethered to the universe itself.

Unlocking your true potential and cosmic light is the ultimate goal in life. You are burdened with a potential that can change the world around you, and by understanding how the human energy systems work, you can fulfill this mission. In this book, we are guided by the energetic components of quantum field theories, morphogenetic field theories, and collective field theories to understand our connection to the cosmic light that flows through us. As Matt 5:14–16 says (*Holy Bible, New International Version*, 2013/1973):

> You are the light of the world. A town built on a hill cannot be hidden. Neither do people light a lamp and put it under a bowl. Instead, they put it on its stand, and it gives light to everyone in the house. In the same way, let your light shine before others, that they may see your good deeds...

This book will take a three-part approach to bring these fundamental truths to life. The three sections are the paradigm of inner and outer space; the divine mind and the realms of consciousness; and the Human Energy Consciousness System. The first part is a scientific and holistic understanding where we explore a paradigm shift in understanding that we are cosmic beings, incarnating into a human experience. I explore the seven stages of incarnation from an energetic perspective of the world we live in from a physiological and spiritual perspective. This establishes the field on which we exist which will help us to build the immediate environment more easily.

The second part then focuses on our mind, that collective mind around us, and the divine mind. Mind can be substituted for infinite intelligence, the source of all knowledge and information. Here, we will see how we are all connected to the phenomenon of the core light, connected to God if you will. This section ends by exploring our own evolution and how it is connected to the spiritual and physiological realms we established earlier.

Lastly, we will get more personal by exploring how our souls move into the physical reality from the core source of life. This part starts with an explanation of incarnation, the movement from the spiritual eternal realm to the finite experience of earth. When we have understood this in light of the complex holographic world we are in, we can then explore our heritage and identity more closely. The end goal, which is the focus of the last few chapters, is to help you understand how the field of information built around you before you even incarnated, has influence on how you let your light shine. The idea of the light will be a recurring theme in all my other books.

I truly believe that we all have blessings, gifts, and talents (according to the parables of Jesus) which we are supposed to bring with our incarnation. The main idea behind this book is helping you understand how these blessings come from your core, how they are constrained as you incarnate, and most importantly, how you can free them to flow in your life. This is why this section will close with a more practical view on how you can create and understand your genogram. As you go through these stages, you are entering into the cosmic web of knowledge, a place where you will connect with the divine and find the best version of yourself.

Cosmic Connections & Transgenerational Patterns

There is an intricate web of connections that binds us all. The patterns etched upon your parental DNA carry echoes of the past, shaping the present reality. You are a unique blend of familial traits, cultural influences, and cosmic energies, all converging to create the essence of who you are.

Your experience of this book will teach you to honor and realize your cosmic essence. You can only embrace your divine purpose with reverence and gratitude and bring the blessings that your light holds into the world if you embrace your divine genogram. Knowing that you are an integral part of the cosmic tapestry allows your light to shine brightly, illuminating the world around you and inspiring others to embrace their cosmic potential.

You are here for a reason. Your incarnation is not random; it is a deliberate weaving of karmic strands and spheres of consciousness. Your existence is a blessing—one that is waiting to unveil itself to the world around you.

Chapter 1:

Inner and Outer Space: A Multidimensional Paradigm

The universe is the energetic fabric from which all consciousness emerges. No matter how different we might appear, every one of us is connected to the same source: the light. To understand who we are completely, we first need to comprehend the intricate and interesting vastness from which we arrived. We have a "DNA signature" that offers vast amount of information to help us understand our origins and purpose for being here. Not only is this strand of DNA based on our ancestors; more than that, it shows the fingerprint of our Creator. This is where you have to start, if you are going to embark on this journey of self-discovery. The infinite universe, God, is the fabric from which we were cut, and by understanding this, we can understand ourselves in turn.

Let's explore the cosmos in all its vastness and beauty by examining the patterns and symmetries that connect the universe to the human energy consciousness system (HECS). The power of the infinite universe and the energy it shares with our bodies will be the key to finding our purpose and place in the world.

Beyond the simple observable expanse of the universe lies an intricate and interconnected framework—one where each celestial body is linked through a complex web, sharing information in ways that defy conventional understanding. This cosmic phenomenon not only connects stars and planets but also entwines the very essence of our minds and consciousness with universal intelligence, hinting at a deeper unity that binds everything together.

This amazing web of life can be witnessed all around us. It's within a blooming flower, a seashell, a forest, a tree, or a mountain range spanning for miles. You can find it within your pet's eyes or in a sea turtle passing by at the beach. The web is everywhere and in everything around you. You are part of this intricate web as well, emerging as your biofield, which is an invisible template for your physical body. You are teeming with so much life and light from the universe.

Our current scientific and spiritual insights provide fascinating glimpses into this grand interconnectedness. Take, for example, quantum entanglement—a phenomenon where particles, regardless of the distance between them, exhibit changes that mirror each other instantaneously. This challenges our traditional notions of space and time, suggesting that something more profound is linking these particles. Similarly, insights from transcendental meditation show us how individual thoughts and emotions resonate within a larger collective field—a concept we will explore further in this book. These instances point to the existence of an invisible informational field, which ancient teachings refer to as the "Flower of Life" or "Sacred Geometry." These systems function outside the limits of physical boundaries, weaving together mind, matter, and the Divine.

In this chapter, we will delve deeper into the concept of interconnectedness, exploring how the evolution of scientific thought, from relativity to quantum physics, has gradually unveiled layers of this intricate web. We will also examine the idea of the universal mind and its connection to divine intelligence. In addition, we will look at the vital role of the human biofield, or the HECS, an invisible system that transports information in various dimensions of existence.

Drawing connections between these realms will shed light on how individual experiences are part of a broader, unified consciousness, offering insights into how we might align ourselves with this universal flow for greater harmony and meaning.

The Holographic Universe A Glimpse Beyond the 3D

Imagine a holographic projector that's a 3D object itself, but it creates a 2D image that floats in midair. The image appears to have depth and detail, but it's ultimately just a projection of light patterns on a flat plane. This is precisely what studies in the holographic universe have shown about our universe. Our entire 3D world is like that projected image: an expression in 3D that comes from the projector. We experience a seemingly solid and deep universe, but the underlying reality could be a vast network of information on a different dimensional "canvas," similar to the flat plane where the holographic image appears.

Think about it this way: When we look at each other and everything else around us, we perceive it as solid and mechanical. However, we know that when we start to break down all the cells and then the atoms that make up everything, at the bottom we will find that everything is made of energy emanating from somewhere. In the same way, the universe would be made of light from the projector, but we would see what that light projects—that is, a solid and natural world.

This is not too hard to conceptualize. As you read this, you are seeing words and numbers that string together to provide information. However, if you are reading this on a digital screen, what you are looking at is light and electrical energy being emitted by the device. Your mind, however, can translate the light on the screen to create words and, from the words, meaning. When you look at your laptop or your phone, you do not see pixels; instead, you see what they represent. Similarly, when we look at the holographic universe, we do not see the light; we see what the light represents.

The idea of the holographic universe originated in the study of black holes. These cosmic wonders are known for their event horizon, a point of no return where gravity is so strong that not even light can escape. According to the laws of thermodynamics, black holes gobble up information; anything that falls in disappears forever. However, this contradicts the principles of quantum mechanics, which state that information and energy cannot be created or destroyed.

Physicists like Gerard 't Hooft and Leonard Susskind have proposed that information isn't truly lost within a black hole but rather encoded on its event horizon, a two-dimensional boundary. In essence, the black hole's interior is somehow "projected" onto its surface. This notion extends beyond black holes, suggesting that our entire 3D universe might be an elaborate projection of information encoded on a lower-dimensional boundary, much like the event horizon of a black hole. We experience a seemingly 3D world, but the underlying reality could be an enormous network of data on a grander, unseen "canvas."

This theory has several implications, including a possible unification of quantum mechanics and general relativity, two of our most successful physical theories that currently have conflicting descriptions of reality. The holographic principle suggests a deeper level where these seemingly disparate theories converge.

This idea is captured well in the work of Jude Currivan, PhD, in her book *The Cosmic Hologram: In-formation at the Center of Creation* (Currivan, 2017). She proposes that our universe operates like a hologram. As explained above, just as a holographic image contains information distributed across its entire surface, our reality may be encoded similarly. However, she extends this idea by explaining that information is more fundamental than energy or matter. Instead of seeing particles as the building blocks of reality, she explores the concept that information is the underlying fabric of the cosmos.

This has important implications for our existence, proposing that we're not just passive observers; we actively participate in shaping reality. Our thoughts, intentions, and awareness contribute to the unfolding of the holographic universe. Everything is interconnected, with each part containing information about the whole. What makes the work of Dr. Currivan interesting is how she draws from quantum physics, cosmology, and other scientific disciplines to support her ideas. I would like to do the same as we explore the divine genogram, so let's look at the evolution of this idea from a scientific perspective, starting back in the early 1990s.

Foundational Ideas
(The Early 1990s)

Gerard 't Hooft (1993) proposed the holographic principle in the context of black holes through his work "Dimensional Reduction in Quantum Gravity." He suggested that information about a black hole's interior could be encoded on its boundary, the event horizon, not lost within it. His work revolutionized our understanding of black holes and became fundamental to the idea of the holographic universe. Hooft's groundbreaking theory sparked a wave of new hypotheses and investigations into the nature of space-time and the fundamental laws of the universe as we know it.

Scientists delved deeper into the implications of the holographic principle and uncovered unexpected connections between black holes, entropy, and quantum mechanics. The idea that the complexity of a black hole's interior could be fully described by information on its surface showed a replication of the holographic theory at a cosmic scale. Researchers grappled with the profound implications of this revelation, contemplating the nature of reality and the underlying structure of space-time.

The holographic principle also raised questions in the scientific world about the nature of information and its preservation in the depths of space. Could the universe itself be akin to a holographic projection, encoding all the information about its contents on a distant surface? The truth is, only the holographic universe theory has the ability to bridge the differences between quantum theory, gravity, and the nature of reality.

Development & Refinement
(The Late 1990s to the Early 2000s)

The involvement of physicist Leonard Susskind in the holographic universe theory began around the same time as that of Gerard 't Hooft, in the early 1990s. While Hooft laid the groundwork, Susskind is credited with significantly developing and refining the theory, particularly through the lens of string theory. Both Hooft and Susskind were working on ideas related to holography and black holes around the early 1990s, but it was in 1995 that Susskind published "The World as a Hologram." This paper detailed his exploration of the holographic principle using string theory and helped solidify the idea within the physics community.

Susskind had the idea that maybe the entire universe could be like a hologram, so he suggested that all the information about our 3D universe is encoded on a higher-dimensional boundary. This higher-dimensional boundary is what I often refer to as "the divine mind" or "the infinite universe." It is from this infinite universe that our world is being projected.

Susskind's work was later improved upon by Juan Maldacena (1998), who discovered the AdS/CFT correspondence, a conjectured relationship between two different physical theories: anti-de Sitter (AdS) space and conformal field theory (CFT). The AdS/CFT correspondence suggests a duality between gravity theories in AdS space-time and gauge theories defined on the boundary of that space-time. This duality provides insights into quantum gravity, black holes, and the nature of space-time itself.

This discovery created a way for scientists to possibly test the holographic principle that Leonard Susskind had proposed. To get a better understanding of this, I want you to imagine that you have had two different puzzles for some time, and then one day you realize that, despite seeming different, they fit together perfectly. Maldacena's work showed that what was happening in the string theory model could be described by the quantum field theory, and vice versa. This correspondence opened up new avenues for physicists to explore the connections between these complex theories more tangibly and practically.

Ongoing Research
(2000s to the Present)

Many physicists are still exploring the implications of the holographic principle, especially the black hole information paradox. The Hawking radiation theory suggests that black holes can slowly lose mass and evaporate over time, leading to the potential loss of information (Hawking, 1974). Although this would not be consistent with the idea that energy cannot be lost or destroyed. If the universe is holographic, then information is not lost but rather saved on the event horizon.

A holographic universe would also help explain some long-standing loopholes in physics, like quantum mechanics and gravity. In addition, it is the theory that best explains the universe's origin and evolution. We know that everything that was created was created at the beginning of everything. No new energy can be created; therefore, all the energy we have now was created at the Big Bang. Now, think of the Big Bang as the projector turning on and sharing what already exists in another realm into this natural world.

A hologram is a kind of consciousness where information is not stored in one place but rather distributed across multiple layers. Each layer could represent a different aspect of the whole. Take, for example, a hologram of a flower. One layer might hold the color data, another the shape, and another the three-dimensionality. Thus, the information being projected can be accessed by the inhabitants of the holographic universe through different levels of consciousness.

These layers are not isolated. They interpenetrate, meaning they influence and inform each other. A change in one layer would ripple through the others, creating a unified and dynamic consciousness—a web of consciousness. We can also visualize these layers as concentric spheres, each representing a different level of awareness within the overall consciousness.

Just like a hologram, where the whole image is contained within each fragment, each layer or sphere could hold the entirety of the consciousness within itself. This reflects the idea of interconnectedness and the potential for any part to access the whole. You may, however, remember that consciousness is a complex phenomenon, and there is more to it than the way in which information is layered around us.

This concept draws parallels with Eastern philosophies that discuss layered realities or the interconnectedness of all things. The most interesting examples are the Akashic records and Carl Jung's collective consciousness theory.

The Multiverse

The possibility that the vast universe we observe is just one of many, each existing in its own realm, has strong foundations in modern scientific theories that we are about to delve into. By exploring multiple realms and universes, I encourage you to contemplate possibilities far beyond your everyday encounters and broaden your perception of existence itself.

In the pursuit of comprehending the universe, scientists have come across something fascinating: the notion of the multiverse. Essentially, contemporary theories propose that what you perceive as "the universe" could be just one among many others. This concept is captured in the theory of the multiverse, but before we delve deeper into the specifics, let's take a moment to admire the structure of our known universe.

You exist in a cosmos governed by four fundamental forces: gravity, electromagnetism, strong nuclear force, and weak nuclear force. These forces function differently depending on the scale, prompting scientists to develop models that classify the universe into various "realms" and "layers." For instance, within our observable universe—spanning from the smallest subatomic particles to the largest galactic clusters—distinct physical laws apply based on the size and composition of the planetary objects being observed.

The concept of information transport helps you see that the universe is an intricate web of interconnected nodes, with each thread representing information flowing seamlessly across different planes of existence. This is how you came to be—as a beam of light traveling from infinity to represent life here on Earth. It's how we all came to be. The connections between these realms aren't bound by the constraints of space and time; instead, they stretch beyond.

So many people have tried to prove the existence of these planes, and the trail they left provides a good understanding of what these realms are and how they function. I believe we exist in a biplanar universe with both a material plane driven by entropy and an information plane driven by negentropy, or negative entropy. This dual system highlights how information is not just a passive entity; it shapes realities, weaving through the fabric of space-time to impact consciousness on multiple levels.

I know this isn't easy to understand, but it is important. So, let's look at an example. Imagine you are standing at the edge of a clear pond and you throw a pebble at the center. The pebble will create ripples, which will travel outward in all directions until they reach the edge of the pond. Now imagine that the edges of the pond represent the different worlds stacked on top of each other. All of them are connected to the center, from which information travels across the world. The ripples touch different points at varying parts of the edge, but they are always linked back to the source. Quantum entanglement provides a scientific glimpse into this phenomenon.

Quantum Entanglement

Quantum entanglement is a phenomenon where particles become interconnected in such a way that the state of one particle instantaneously affects the state of another, regardless of the distance separating them. This was first observed and recorded by Einstein and his colleagues in the 1930s (Einstein et al., 1935). Upon making this discovery, Einstein was skeptical of the concept, believing it contradicted the principles of locality and realism in physics. He gave it the name "spooky action at a distance," because the observation was hard to reconcile with the scientific framework as it was understood at that time. Einstein proposed that the theory was incomplete, as the information seemed to travel from one particle to the other faster than any known mode could allow.

In response to this, Erwin Schrödinger exchanged a couple of letters with Einstein trying to prove the validity and completeness of the theory. He came up with the term "entanglement" to describe the quantum states of interconnected particles and used the famous Schrödinger's cat to explain the superposition state of the cat.

Schrödinger explored how entangled particles could exhibit correlations in their measurements even when separated, emphasizing the inherent nonlocality of quantum mechanics and challenging long-standing intuitions about the behavior of distant objects. His work laid the foundation for much of modern quantum theory and our understanding of how particles can remain connected across vast distances. This connection showed that information could be transmitted from one particle to another through methods different from those that are common in the materialistic view of the world. This phenomenon hints that information might not be limited by physical separation, suggesting a deeper level of interconnectivity affecting not just particles but potentially minds and souls as well.

In quantum entanglement, particles become invisibly linked together. These linked particles act as one, sharing a bond that makes them behave in sync no matter the distance between them. Scientists have a hard time accepting and understanding this discovery, but the evidence is solid.

This is also happening at a more spiritual level. Our individual experiences are not isolated but interwoven with the collective consciousness. Just as a single neuron fires differently based on its network, our thoughts and feelings reverberate through a larger cosmic orchestra. Maharishi Mahesh Yogi's insights into transcendental consciousness further emphasize this connection. By focusing inward and experiencing unity, individuals can break free from the cycles of duality that breed conflict and fear (Maharishi Mahesh Yogi, 1967).

Let's think about this. Quantum entanglement suggests that

particles and photons can be entangled and exist in a place where they are able to transfer information outside of the laws of space and time. This is interesting because our bodies—mine and yours—are made up of cells, which in turn are made up of atoms, which can be broken down into electrons and photons. This means we are made up of energy; we are all energy, which is built with DNA to create what we then perceive as our bodies.

However, if we are energy at our core, what does that say about our ability to be entangled with each other? Does this mean we become nodes, each one part of the intricate design of the universe and with a special part to play? Yes, that is exactly the implication. You are a node on the Tree of Life, and you have both a source that you are connected to and a purpose for existing. Your potential, however, is tied up in understanding that you are part of something bigger than you perceive. We will explore this concept when we go over the chakra system later in the book. We all emit frequencies that impact each other and create different expressions of the Flower of Life. The chakra system is therefore an information transport system, emerging from our core essence and appearing here, holographically, in the Earth plane.

The information transport system is then pivotal in shaping your experiences and the collective consciousness. Have you ever had moments where a sudden insight or idea seemed to pop out of nowhere, perhaps while meditating or during a quiet walk? Those instances might be direct results of this ongoing information exchange, where your consciousness taps into broader streams of cosmic intelligence. The transport of information forms the backbone of this interconnected web, making it indispensable for understanding ourselves and the universe at large.

An easier way for you to understand this is by thinking about what happens when you dream, especially when you enter a lucid state during your dreams. Where does the information you perceive come from, and why are you able to access it only when you are sleeping? Could it be that we have always had this connection to other realms but often only realize it when we are sleeping, because that is when the parts of our minds that are not limited by the constraint of this reality come alive?

I certainly think so. Beyond that, understanding what these realms are and how we can improve our connection to them will help you understand who you are and what your purpose on Earth is. The existence of an energy system sets the foundation for understanding the network of cosmic intelligence from which you arrived into this world.

The two main theories we have for understanding our world—relativity and quantum physics—have shown us that reality isn't as straightforward as it seems. Einstein's theories of relativity introduced us to a curved space-time that bends under the weight of mass and energy, while quantum physics revealed a world that defies logic, where particles exist in superpositions and can be entangled across galaxies.

Science itself has been challenging the way we think about time, space, and matter; at first glance, it might seem like it is pulling away the very foundations on which our reality relies. When you think about it, though, you realize that these discoveries pull away not the foundations of our reality but the misconceptions we have accepted, thereby revealing the truth about who we are and what life is like.

Now more than ever, you need to peek through the cracks that science has left in the ground and find the truth about your being. There, you will see a light that will blind you to the mundane and dull representation of reality but open you up to the potential within you—the energy that you incarnated into this plane to bear and share with the world. You are the light of the world, a city on a hill. But you need to understand that light to manifest it in this world.

Once you understand and accept that you are part of something bigger than yourself, you will start to see how all the different elements of your life tie back to the energy field that holographically exists through you. It is the light inside you that can then be channeled to bring healing to the situations and people around you. It's that same light that you can emanate to change the energy in your life and in the lives of the people you care about. You are so full of potential, the incarnation of the pure light and love of the universe. I have no greater pleasure in life than seeing more and more people inspired by the realization of the potential they hold within.

We are yet to open the veil of conventional understanding, though, and we need to keep building on the ideas we have explored in this chapter. The main goal is to help you understand who you are and where you come from. We have gone over the intricate setup of our universe first, because you can never understand yourself until you understand the whole. You are an apple from the Tree of Life, and you have to understand the tree to understand yourself.

We are all like fruits on a tree in more profound ways than we think. We develop within the tree, then we emerge out of flowers into bright fruits that fill the tree for a season. At some point, however, we will fall off the tree and return to being seeds, before being reborn as new trees.

In this chapter, we have examined how our ideas about our universe as a physical and mechanical world are shaky. Instead, the foundations of everything are governed by scientific rules whose implications challenge everything we know about ourselves.

The way quantum particles behave is a problem scientists are still trying to solve. We know that everything we have now is built from the energy of the Big Bang. The light exploded into quarks and photons, which eventually made up everything we see and know. We know from the laws of quantum physics discussed above that once atoms are connected, they will always stay connected regardless of distance and time. This means that every action on one atom shares information with the rest of the connected atoms. If we follow this, we learn something important: We are all matter, we are all made out of the same quarks and photons, and we have all been connected since the inception of time.

Let's move on and build on that idea. Now that we know we are all joined in some way, let's talk about the divine mind in the next chapter and consider just how connected we are.

Chapter 2:
The Divine Mind and the Realms of Consciousness

Let's go back in time to 13th-century Spain to explore how the kabbalistic concept of Kether emerged. Kabbalah is an ancient tradition that originated from the teachings of sages in Jewish mysticism. Its ideas have informed most modern-day science, and most religions as well; I know it will also be able to help you understand the mysteries of the universe, the soul, and the relationship between the physical and the metaphysical realms. Over time, Kabbalah has evolved and branched into various schools of thought and practices, such as the Lurianic Kabbalah and the Hasidic Kabbalah. Through all of this, though, the fundamental revelation of these beliefs still provides great insight into the universal mind and the divine mind.

Kabbalah references the Tree of Life—the same one that we find in the book of Genesis in the Bible. The Tree of Life symbolizes how the Infinite manifested the material world. At the top is Kether, symbolizing the divine mind, unity, and the source of creation. Kether is the highest of the divine realms and has been referred to by many different names in different traditions. It is what Paul called the "seventh heaven," the part of Heaven where God lives. This realm contains the purest form of divine consciousness and is where everything begins and ends. Yes, that includes you; this is where your light incarnated from.

Since Kether is bound by neither time nor space, this means you have always existed in the past, present, and future, and exist in the latter in a state of energy that is not subject to the laws that bind this current reality. However, you chose to have your light manifest in this world, bound by space and time, when you moved through the vortex of interdimensional space that connects the different dimensions to appear in your mother's womb.

The Universal & Divine Mind

Buried within the beautiful discoveries of Kabbalah is the idea of the universal mind, a consciousness that is not local to anyone specifically. This would be like an infinite intelligent mind that exists on its own and intricately connects to everyone and everything in the known and unknown universe. In the same way that all our body parts are connected to and inform our mind, we are all like parts that inform and interact with the universal mind.

Think about how your mind interacts with your body. It responds when there is pain in your leg, and it shares that information with your hand so it can attend to your leg. Simultaneously, your eyes are directed to focus on the same leg to see if anything is going on that might need attention. In the same way, we are all giving feedback to the universe, and the universe is giving us information back. We are then connected just like the nodes in our brain are, and the relationships we create become like neural connections in the brain.

The interconnectedness of the universal mind influences our thoughts and experiences along with the collective consciousness of humanity as a whole. This shared consciousness may explain how certain ideas or inventions seem to manifest simultaneously in different parts of the world, suggesting a deeper connection beyond our physical boundaries. We are not isolated beings but rather integral parts of a vast, interconnected web of existence that transcends the limitations of the individual self. By tapping into this universal consciousness, you can access profound insights and wisdom that can guide you toward a greater understanding of yourself and your place in this world.

Let's delve deeper into the implications of the universal mind and explore how our thoughts and intentions have the power to shape not only our reality but also the collective reality we all partake in. I believe this comes with a challenge to take responsibility for the energy we contribute to this shared consciousness. You are powerful, and you can change and affect the collective consciousness with your energy. By aligning your intentions and actions with the flow of the universal mind, you might find yourself a co-creator of a more peaceful and enlightened world, where compassion and understanding take center stage.

One way the universal mind and our interconnectedness can help you become your best is through inspiration and intuition. I believe that moments of sudden insight or creative brilliance are not solely the products of individual minds but rather gifts from the universal consciousness with which we are all intertwined. Opening yourself up to this expansive source of creativity and wisdom helps you tap into a limitless wellspring of innovative ideas and solutions that transcend the boundaries of conventional thinking. Cultivating a receptive state of mind that is attuned to the whispers of the universal mind can lead you down paths of discovery and innovation that you may never have imagined possible on your own.

This all brings us back to exploring the nature of reality itself, and our place within the vastness of existence. The interconnectedness you sense with all living beings and the cosmos is not merely a metaphorical concept but a fundamental truth of our shared reality. This reality is not built on the world that we experience physically, though, but is a realm that exists at a different frequency. That we are all integral parts of a grander whole suggests a profound unity that transcends the divisions and separations we often perceive in our daily lives. It is possible to find solace in the understanding that we are never truly alone but rather inseparable threads in the intricate fabric of universal consciousness.

The concept of the universal mind offers us a paradigm-shifting perspective on the nature of reality and our interconnectedness with all that exists. Tethered to the existence of the universal mind, however, is the idea of the divine mind, a higher intelligence or consciousness that is transcendental and all-knowing. Some call this divine mind God, some simply call it the universe, but I like to use the wording "infinite universe." There is a vastness and transcendence to God that offers you direction and guidance as you journey through this realm. As this realm informs you of your journey, you are being authored by this infinite intelligent universe. The divine design of our life is interwoven in the very fabric of our existence.

It's the guidance of the infinite universe that helps us find the knowledge of who we are even after incarnation has happened. The change from our state of light to physical beings on this Earth gives us a new childlike spiritual mind that can rediscover its identity. In the same way that a child learns about their physical body, learning to crawl, stand, and then walk, your spirit can also learn about who you are within. The more you learn, the more you will understand the light within you and how it operates.

We are energy that exists as if in a beehive, and that beehive is divine. This divinity starts with the unlimited universe itself and moves to us. The light that we are as part of the unlimited universe then travels to the Earth, and our souls find a home within our bodies. However, although we are under the illusion that we have left these realms behind, it is our birthright to experience them. We still have the ability, through knowledge and application, to access the realms that are holographically interwoven aspects of our innate consciousness. This looks like a window into time and space. In later chapters, we will delve into how these realms are available to us not as physical beings but as cosmic souls that can move out of time and space. In the next section, we will explore the idea of the existence of different spheres and realms.

Realms of Consciousness

It can be very difficult to conceptualize how different realms can exist at the same time and in the same space, so let's start with an example. Imagine a cardboard box with a thin plastic lining on the inside and a foil lining on the outside. When you place food inside the box, it is technically in a foil box, but it is just as much in a cardboard box and also in a plastic container. You exist in a similar box. There are multiple realms, all of which you are in at the same time. While you only see the physical world when you look around you, that does not mean this is the only reality you exist within. The plastic that lines the inside of the box is what you would see if you were in it, in which case you might fail to realize it also has the integrity that cardboard brings and the insulation that the foil provides.

We are the same way ourselves: We exist in this physical world as physical beings, but we are also energy existing in another place at the same time. If you start to understand this about your existence, you can begin to access these other realms and the knowledge they have for you.

As humanity, we know that multiple levels of consciousness exist and that they all have an effect on the world in which we live. The divine universe is different from the networks we have here on Earth, so it has to exist outside of what we can perceive. In the same way, the divine mind cannot interact within this physical realm as it exists out of time and space. Through the years, we have tried our best to explain what these realms are, and this has created fairly reliable multifaceted views. While the aesthetics of the realms are different from one group of people to the next, their existence and operation are very similar. Let's look at the unique ways in which some people have defined these spiritual realms that our souls are a part of.

Examples of Realms of Consciousness

Christianity is grounded on the existence of realms in the same way that the energy system is grounded throughout and along our bodies. Just as the third eye is at the center of our forehead and is connected to spiritual energy and to the divine mind, so is the highest Heaven and the place that God abides. In Christianity, this realm is referred to as the spiritual world, where angels abide, while the Earth plane or material world is where humans live. The material realm is like a schoolhouse and a temporary residence for learning. Just as the physical body is a place our energy body illuminates for a time, it is only temporary. We are here for a while and then our energy leaves our bodies as we return to the realm out of time and space.

Heaven is the divine plane where we will all live after this life has passed. Throughout the Bible, it is referred to as "home." In one instance, Jesus says that in His Father's house, there are many rooms to live in, and He invites all the disciples to live with Him when their time on Earth is up.

Interestingly, in Christianity there is also a demarcation made between Heaven and Hell. Both represent the polarity of entering the physical world, bringing the opposites of these two worlds into balance. One is full of goodness and light, while the other is full of suffering. As our mission while on Earth is to learn to be a blessing of light, to emanate our light to transform, transcend, and ultimately transfigure human suffering into light, and to give our light and energy a chance to grow in line with the divine will, it follows that our afterlife will be somewhat affected by how well we steward this current life.

I truly believe we came as a blessing of light into this world. We incarnate with the full intention of helping the evolution of humanity, only to be trapped by one of the realms of suffering, trauma, or emotional and cognitive pollution. Accordingly, if you remember the light within and heal past trauma, thereby changing your frequency and transmission, you fully incarnate as a blessing to this world. While reincarnation might not be as tragic as Hell, it follows that you will do better if you listen and follow a deeper calling, spending your time on Earth aligned with your divine purpose rather than blinded to it.

There are other realms in addition to the Christian ones, such as the six realms in Buddhism. Unlike the two Christian realms, stacked on top of and below the Earth we live on, Buddhism says that the six realms, also known as the six paths, are intricately interconnected with states of consciousness and influenced by the law of karma. These realms include different states of existence, including heavenly realms, where beings experience joy and tranquility; the human realm, characterized by duality and moral choices; the animal realm, with primal instincts; the hungry ghost realm, depicting insatiable desires; the Hell realm, of retribution and suffering; and the Asura (demigod) realm, where power struggles define existence.

In Hindu philosophy, the idea of lokas or talas embodies various planes of existence inhabited by diverse entities that transcend the earthly realm. These planes represent distinct spheres of reality and house deities, celestial beings, humans, and other entities. In contrast, in Japanese folklore there is Yomi, which refers to the land of the dead or the underworld. It is the realm where the dead reside and is commonly associated with darkness and gloom. While Yomi is associated with the underworld, it is also where departed souls find their resting place.

Moreover, the spiritual beliefs of Native American traditions also acknowledge a myriad of spiritual realms interwoven with the natural world. These realms are inhabited by spirits, ancestors, and supernatural beings, coexisting harmoniously with the earthly realm. Through rituals, ceremonies, and storytelling, Native American communities honor and celebrate the interconnectedness of the physical and spiritual dimensions, fostering a deep reverence for the unseen forces that shape their collective existence.

The rich history of all cultures guides us to a tapestry of the infinite universe that leads us all toward a unified home of oneness. These traditions have found a way to connect and interact with different levels of consciousness that have always existed. Now, we will explore the seven stages of incarnation and how these realms impact your life and mission here on Earth. Let's begin by looking at an underlying theory that supports the idea of an interconnected conscious universe as a memory field.

Akashic Records & Collective Consciousness

Ervin László's work introduced the Akashic field, an idea that clarifies the consequences of the holographic universe like no other. In his book Science and the Akashic Field, László argues that there is an interconnected cosmic field known as the Akashic record, which mystics and sages believe conserves and conveys information about reality (László, 2007). Recent findings in vacuum physics suggest that this Akashic field corresponds to science's zero-point field, the foundation of space itself (Baksa, 2011).

This helped verify László's work, which posited that the Akashic field is a subtle energy matrix from which everything in the universe emerges, connecting atoms, galaxies, living beings, and consciousness. He brings forward the integral "theory of everything" that unifies modern science with ancient spiritual traditions, illustrating the interconnectedness of existence—an interconnectedness we will use to help you improve your productivity, self-awareness, creativity, and efficiency in fulfilling your tasks here on Earth.

I love the convergence that has emerged from László's work. The unity of the different viewpoints from religion to science will help us get a clearer understanding of what this unified memory is. The Akashic field—or, as László calls it, the A-field—is a feature found in many religions and belief systems. Think about the concept of the Kiraman Katibin in Islam, two angels who record your actions, thoughts, and feelings throughout the day. Their name translates to "honorable recorders" or "noble writers."

Christianity talks about the recording of all our actions while we are here on Earth and how we will be accountable for them after this life. The idea that everything that is happening is part of the great web of information recorded about everyone and everything is beautiful. In the same way that you are everlasting, so is the A-field and the information it contains.

This holographic informational field is being shared around the universe faster than the speed of light and it has a direct effect on everyone and everything in the universe. This means that our actions have rippling effects that are felt instantaneously throughout the universe. As we move and act in the world, we help to shape it into what it is, and it interacts with us in return and influences who we become.

Later, we will explore real-life examples of how we interact with this field of information through our biofields, which are like the receptors, distributors, and processors of such information. Since the information cannot be received by any of the five senses that our bodies rely on, there is a special field around each of us that is capable of understanding the information in the A-field and learning about the world through it.

For now, let's explore the idea of the A-field, or the zero-point Akashic field, being the enduring memory of the universe, retaining records of all past and future events on Earth and beyond. By bridging the gap between science and spirituality, we can highlight the deep unity underlying creation, reinforcing the idea that, while we may seem isolated like islands on the surface, we are fundamentally interconnected: in the depths of our existence.

You should rethink your perception of the universe, as our world is not confined to the definitions provided by science, religion, or any other philosophy. All these are parts of the whole, but we need a holistic view that transcends conventional boundaries. László, just like I do, had an extensive background in philosophy, systems theory, and future studies; this enriches his narrative, lending credibility to his exploration of the Akashic field and its implications for human understanding. This multifaceted nature is crucial if we are going to unlock the divine genome within every person.

Because the Akashic records are like a giant database of human experiences, when we connect with a particular realm within the Akashic records, we are tuning into a specific set of memories and energies associated with that realm. I want you to think of the A-field as the field of neurological connections in your brain. There are over 100 billion neurons and over 100 trillion synaptic connections in your brain, each helping to create different ideas and actions as you wish (*Colón-Ramos Lab*, n.d.). As you think, different parts of your brain become active depending on what you are thinking about. Your brain leads your body to get into a specific mode depending on the thoughts you are having.

This is why you physically feel emotional pain: Your body is connected and wired by the specific conditions in your brain at the time. When you are concentrating on an idea, your brain connections rearrange to focus on that concept. This is why meditation and affirmations work. If you think about something long enough, you condition your body and frame of mind to act like that thought is a reality. The thought influences the outcome in the physical space.

Now, let's correlate this to the A-field. Imagine the A-field is a brain, and it has the memory and the entire knowledge of all of existence. Every time someone has smiled, cried, felt betrayed, or been happy, their emotions have been captured in this universal brain. Just like the human brain, different areas of the A-field will light up depending on what the collective group of people are doing or thinking about, so you can access different layers and consciousness levels in the unified memory.

Here's a thought before we move forward: Have you ever asked yourself why, despite our differences in culture and tradition, we have very similar understandings of things like emotions and feelings? Carl Jung referred to this as the collective consciousness: "shared, inherited unconscious knowledge and experiences across generations, expressed through universal symbols and archetypes common to all human cultures" (McLeod, 2024, "Collective Unconsciousness" para 1).

The idea that even in our differences we keep converging in how we represent ideas is phenomenal. Let's look at a few examples of this and how they show a connectedness that transcends our current reality and points to a deeper connection. Below is a collection of ideas from the past that are stored and transmitted to each successive generation:

- the circle: represents unity, wholeness, and infinity
- the Tree of Life: symbolizes the connection between all forms

of creation and knowledge

- the mandala: represents the universe and harmony
- the phoenix: represents rebirth and renewal
- the hero: embodies the journey of overcoming obstacles and achieving greatness
- the mother: symbolizes nurturing, creation, and the cycle of life
- the wise old man or woman: represents wisdom, guidance, and knowledge
- the yin and yang symbol: represents balance and harmony
- the infinity sign: symbolizes eternity, universality, and the interconnectedness of all things

These symbols and archetypes resonate deeply within the collective unconscious, connecting individuals across cultures and eras. If you study the above symbols in any culture, you will likely find variations with the same meaning.

I will show you only two concepts that are similar across cultures, but I encourage you to study beyond this and find others as well. For starters, let's look at the dragon and consider the following representations from different traditions and cultures: Nyami Nyami (Zimbabwe), Fáfnir (Scandinavia), Lóng (China), Ninki Nanka (West Africa), Quetzalcoatl (Central America), Griffin (Mediterranean and Middle East), and the Bakunawa (The Philippines). The existence of such a mythological creature across so many different cultures is interesting. I know some scientists have tried to disprove the connection with the idea that these are all inspired by the discovery of dinosaur skeletons, but this is not true for most of the regions on that list (*6 Mythical Dragons*, 2023).

Another idea we can consider is the son of God who is half-human and who comes to Earth to fulfill his mission. You can see this motif in the stories of people like Krishna from India,

Osiris of Egypt, Tien of China, and countless others. In the book *The World's Sixteen Crucified Saviors*, we can see another motif of this ultimate sacrifice across many different cultures as well (Graves, 1875).

There is a problem, however, with how we frame these stories today, but this can easily be solved by understanding the A-field, or our interconnectedness. The issue is that we think these stories are exclusive, meaning if one is true, then none of the other ones can be. Each culture tries to gatekeep their own revelation from the rest of the world and believes that all other instances of the same motif must be false or a copy of their original. This lie stands to bring down the truth that we are all the same and connected to the center of it all, regardless of how we perceive that truth.

The truth is not in one religion, nor in one view that science holds, nor in one tradition. It is embedded in a transcended cloud of information that informs all of these fields. If you take quantum science and try to use it to explain how huge objects like planets work, you will fall into a contradiction. The same is true if you try to apply Newton's laws to quarks and photons. This does not mean either is false—not at all—but they tap into the knowledge of the universe at different scales.

This is why it's important to understand the A-field and the collective consciousness before you imagine creating your divine genogram. The quality that makes you unique and divine is also found in everyone else, because we are all part of the same source: the universal infinite mind.

The A-field leads us smoothly back to consciousness. Let's go back to the example of brain waves. I want you to imagine that each configuration of the neurons in your mind is a level of consciousness. Consciousness is how aware you are about something. In the case of life, consciousness refers to how aware you are of your existence, but you can be conscious about many other areas of your life. Imagine each neuron has its own consciousness and purpose to transmit signals of information across a whole system.

Have you ever had an experience that completely changed how

you see the world? Maybe you were in a car accident and survived, but now every time you get into a car, you become aware of the possibility of another crash, and you strap on your seat belt. Or maybe it's something else, like a relationship that made you see trust differently. These stored memories provide up-to-date information or signal anxiety depending on how the event was mapped in your memory system and nervous system. Now, these configurations in your brain and your consciousness levels can influence how you act and think.

We know from research that if you lock into a specific level of consciousness, you can be so consumed by it that you lose awareness of everything else around you. An experiment by Chabris & Simons (2011) looked at attention and how we can move into states where our minds turn everything off, keeping us focused on the pertinent issue. In the experiment, run at Harvard University, several students were shown a video of a couple of students passing a ball around. In the video, half the students were wearing black while the other half were wearing white. The observers were tasked with counting how many times the ball was passed between the players in white. In the middle of the video, however, a man in a full gorilla costume walks into the frame, beats his chest like a gorilla would, and then walks off out of the frame.

At the end of the video, the observers were asked how many times the ball had been passed around, and almost everyone got that right. However, when asked if they had seen the gorilla, half of them had no idea what was being referred to. Despite this being something you would not miss if you were just watching the video without having to focus on the white team, you could easily miss it if you were assigned this specific task.

You can choose the configuration of neurological connections that controls your life, but, even more than that, you can choose the configuration of memories in the A-field that controls your life. Since the A-field is like your brain, it has specific consciousness levels that configure specific collections of feelings and states of being.

The Akashic records vibrate at their unique frequency. When you resonate with a specific realm within the Akashic field, you are attuning yourself to that frequency, which allows you to access the memories and energies stored within it. It's like tuning a radio to a particular station to listen to a specific type of music. Now think of the implications of connecting to a negative realm—anger, perhaps. You would be allowing the collective memory of that negative frequency to be a part of you and control how you act and make decisions.

Fortunately, the result is the same if you tap into a positive realm, like trust or love. When you tap into a specific realm within the Akashic field, you will find yourself influenced by the events and emotions linked to that realm. It's like stepping into a room filled with echoes of the past, where the reverberations of historical events and feelings linger in the air. You open yourself up to the experiences and emotions that have been imprinted within whichever realm you are in.

Realms are a very important concept with serious implications for our lives. Imagine what would happen if you ever reached a time where you were living in the reality of the fullness of your light, your core dimension—if you tapped into the higher realms and released yourself from the levels of consciousness that block your light from radiating through.

Lower Realms as States of Consciousness

The seven lower realms, once considered sins—greed, gluttony, wrath, lust, sloth, pride, and envy—are seen as moral failures more than anything else, but could there be more to these seemingly universally acknowledged failings? By envisioning them as spheres or realms of consciousness that exist holographically and interweave with our consciences, we can delve into the depths of our psyche and understand how they affect us.

The seven lower realms represent habits and behaviors that pull us away from the light, but most people associate them with failure and judgment. This is not what we will be talking about in this section, though; I do not want you to feel judged or at fault as we go through these sins, so we will refer to them as harmful habits or negative actions.

The seven states of consciousness create emotional and cognitive pollution that detours us away from the light within. Paradoxically, this leads us back to the light when we are humbled by our suffering and realize how much we need to seek a higher power and surrender our egoic struggles.

To best understand this, I want you to think about consciousness as awareness or attention. If you are conscious of your body, then you are aware of it and you give it attention. You act in ways that reflect that awareness, allowing it to shape how you think and see the world. For example, if you are insecure about your body and conscious about it, you will wear clothes that help cover up the parts you are not so proud of; when you are in public, you will think that everyone is looking at you.

Now, consider what your experience would be if you were connected to the light within. You would act like every moment on Earth is an opportunity to share your light with the people around you. You would naturally shine your light so that all those around you could sense and feel it and be inspired to live in their own radiance.

Your light will manifest to the world differently depending on your task on Earth, but regardless, we all have a divine message that our souls need to accomplish. Everyone is special and carries something that the world is in great need of. Maybe for you, this is art, divine love, new inventions, or something within your line of work. Whatever it is, as soon as your consciousness is committed to your mission, you will be unstoppable.

The fullness of your creativity, energy, and productivity is waiting for you in a higher state of consciousness. When you connect your local mind to the divine mind and start to draw from the infinite universe, you will become conscious of your divine mission. I like to think of it as an astronaut mission. Imagine you get sent into space with a mission on one of the satellites and, when you get there, you have to perform several tasks. You will do these tasks better if you keep your connection to the team on Earth open and communicate the whole way through. The team can give you feedback, guidance, and information that you will need to make your job easier and more efficient.

It is the same with your mission here on Earth: Your soul has a mission to fulfill, and to do this, it has to be connected to the flow of information and light from the infinite universe. Only then will you be able to fulfill the assignment that you and your spirit guides agreed on before you incarnated here. So, here comes the big question: What stops us from believing in our calling? What keeps us from connecting to the higher levels of consciousness? What inhibits us from receiving the flow of information from the infinite intelligent universe?

The answer is a couple of things, most of which we will explore in the coming chapters, among which are the lower realms of consciousness that trap us in repeated patterns. These habits act like nets that capture our attention and block the proper flow of energy into our being. I love listening to how we use figures of speech, which when you think about it are not just "figures of speech" but often truths and realities we do not yet fully understand. I bring this up because when we refer to the seven challenges, we often say things like, "I was overtaken by anger [wrath] and just couldn't stop myself," or, "You're so blinded by lust that you cannot see that what you are doing is harmful to yourself."

Let's think about it: Why do these habits overtake, control, possess, hijack, or seize us? Better yet, what part of us do they possess? It is not our physical bodies, as there are no physical restraints on us. Here is the reality: The seven habits are like holographic realms that interact with our energy and in which we can get stuck and overtaken. It's never just a figure of speech—the habits keep us in a lower consciousness, where we are no longer aware of our divine qualities, and we spiral deeper and deeper into the negative reality those habits create for us. In a later chapter, we will explore how these habits can be tied to your family history and transmitted to you, as well as how you can free yourself from them and allow your light and energy to flow through unhindered again.

Needless to say, the human condition is complex and woven

with threads of virtue alongside these vices we need to escape. The seven harmful habits transcend mere moral failings and represent fundamental aspects of our consciousness, existing holographically and interpenetrating our very being.

There is an invisible Akashic memory field, as introduced by László, that records all events, thoughts, and feelings. There are also frequency bands of anger, fear, grief, joy, and prayers that all interpenetrate and impact us.

Multidimensional Paradigm

Stop, take a moment to breathe, and think about everything we have discussed so far. Close your eyes for a moment, and imagine that your essence exists not only in this world but is spread out across multiple levels. Keeping your eyes closed as you think about this, imagine that you have been to another realm before, and that you entered this world from that realm. The mind is a powerful tool that can help you picture and conceptualize the concepts we have covered.

The idea of other realms existing is evident in both science and religion. The implications of quantum entanglement and ideas like string theory point to worlds that do not function in the same way as our own, and that the world we live in is only an expression and experience.

The idea that you are a blessing of light and are innately divine is your birthright. It is echoed in so many mythological narratives from the past. The archetype of the half-God who comes to the human realm and proves himself can be traced closely to stories like those of Thor and Hercules. Both of these heroes are sons of God in their narratives, children of the divine mind, but they each leave the splendor of their father's realm to come to Earth. Both of them prove themselves through this exercise and are given a higher status at the end.

Now, beyond the stories of Thor and Hercules, we also have the story of Jesus Christ of Nazareth, another God who came to Earth and took on human form so he could go through life virtuously and ascend to a higher rank at the end.

I know that when we read these stories, we often consider them as just that—stories. But think about it for a moment—the coincidence that there would be such a striking resemblance between narratives that were crafted by different people at different times in history is uncanny. Here is a possible solution to reconcile this: There is a reason why the earthly realm is always in the middle and the rest are on top and at the bottom.

In the following chapter, I introduce the seven stages of incarnation. We will explore how the HECS forms before your physical incarnation, and how you enter through the astral realms and Akashic field of the Earth plane. I will show that incarnation happens through the chakra points in the body, which are like vortexes that allow energy to move from one realm to another—in this case, from the astral world to this natural world. The reason this is so, is that incarnation is the miracle through which you enter the Earth's world, the human realm. Just as all those other cosmic wonders left the realm out of time and space to come to Earth and experience its good and bad, you too have done the same.

The Bible says that Jesus was the light of the world and then he became a man and dwelt among us (*Holy Bible, New International Version*, 2013/1973, John 1). In the same way, you too have been a light, and now you have come to dwell among others on Earth. I know this idea is mind-boggling, but the blueprint that supports it is solid. You are a blessing of light and have a calling to illuminate the world and to live according to the Divine here on Earth.

Chapter 3:

Human Energy Consciousness System

To cognize the Divine Essence—this is the highest purpose of the soul, sent by the Creator to the Earth! –Pythagoras

It is very easy to feel defeated and overwhelmed, especially in this age. So many people have their divineness suppressed by the worries of this world, trauma, and lower-consciousness vibrations like the seven harmful behaviors we discussed in the previous chapter. The human condition can grip us so tightly, making us forget that we have a divine purpose and a divine origin whose potential is waiting to shine through.

I know it can be difficult to see that there is more to life than the mundane activities that often have us in loops, going through the same cycles day after day. So many people wake up with no excitement for the day and drag themselves through it, just so they can get to the end and sleep, only to wake up and repeat the pattern. This is not what we were designed to do, though; we are so much more than we might realize when our energy has been dampened and we have lost connection to our divine roots.

The most dangerous thing in life is convincing ourselves that we are nothing special and that there is nothing to us but the world we live in and experience. I am here to convince you otherwise: You are a blessing, you have a purpose, and you are eternal. According to Pythagoras and other wisdom traditions, your incarnation is part of a great migration of souls that have been traveling to and from this planet since its inception (Luchte, 2009).

You might not know it right now, especially as you may not remember the source of your divinity, but you came here by choice, and you have a purpose that you are meant to fulfill. Not only that, you have what it takes to find your place in this interconnected world and make a difference. I love talking about how I found my divine mission to help others discover their light and how it has brought so much meaning to my life.

In high school, I was influenced by an English elective class on Synchronicity by Carl Jung. Later, I was guided to read books by Carlos Castaneda, Paramahansa Yogananda, and Ruth Montgomery. Then, in my search for self and untangling the mystery around my birth, in 1987 I was handed Barbara Brennan's self-published book, *Hands of Light: A Guide Through the Human Energy Field.* This book seemed to provide scientific answers to many of my questions about the invisible phenomena I had experienced as a child. It all made sense. Those foundational experiences were the seeds that guided my path toward remembering my divine purpose and my joy in sharing these insights with you. Perhaps sharing them will awaken a spark that guides your own inquiry and curiosity.

Let's explore another inspiring tale that shows how God is the author of your life regardless of the situation you were born into. In my journey, I discovered the truth about who I am, the world we live in, and the interconnectedness that binds everything together. From my experiences and explorations, I have grown to understand the secrets of the universe and the human biofield—especially how they can help you discover who you are and how to walk in your light. I have shared my story already, so now, let's consider another from history that carries the same ideas.

A young man lived a couple of thousand years ago at the height of the Mesopotamian civilization. He grew up with his foster parents, who told him they had found him alone in the forest when he was young. The family was very poor and raised him to survive in their harsh conditions. The family lived far from the main city, but now and then the boy would travel there to sell the produce of the land that he and his family had worked so hard on.

One day, however, when the boy was older, he was arrested in the city and brought before the King. He had been accused of stealing while selling the produce from the farm. When he was before the King, the boy refused to confess to the crimes, as he had not stolen anything. The King believed him, and instead of having him jailed, he ordered that the boy be stripped and whipped five times on the back.

When the boy had been stripped, however, the King ordered the guards to stop before they could whip the boy, and he and his Queen stood up and walked down to where the boy was standing. They looked at the mark over his left shoulder, a mark they recognized. Immediately, the King asked the boy who his parents were. When the boy told the King about how he had been found alone in the forest when he was a boy, the King and Queen knew he was their long-lost son.

You see, the King and Queen had lost their first son in a forest years ago after being ambushed on their way to a wedding in another city. They had never seen the boy again, and always assumed he had been killed by the beasts of the forest. But now here he was, their son. They covered him up and quickly had him brought into the castle to live with them. He was celebrated and put in a position of great power as the Prince. From here, he was able to help his adoptive parents as well and used his influence and power to bring justice to people all over the land.

I do not want you to see this as an isolated story, though. The idea that we are seeking our true identities echoes throughout history, and it remains important now. The story above is an example of a greater archetypal plot that exists in your life and mine today. That is what narratives and stories do—they present the truths that we are grappling to understand as entertainment. The reason we understand and embrace these forms of media, however, is primarily because they speak to a truth in which we already exist.

History tells a story of the great odyssey of humanity: our quest for self-discovery, and how we arrive here on Earth and leave an impact before we move on to allow others to also bring their light. Pythagoras told this narrative, likening Earth to a station to which thousands of souls are migrating and that thousands are leaving. It makes you think of airline travel, as well as how we have people leaving and arriving all the time, corresponding to the 350,000 births and 250,000 deaths we have each day on Earth (Big Think, 2014).

The human experience will always be one of inquiry. Who are we, and where did we come from? What are we, and what can we become? Physicist and futurist Dr. Michio Kaku shared how the idea that we could at some point exist as pure consciousness roaming the cosmos is a physical possibility. We have always been part of universal consciousness. This is where my current belief arises that we are cosmic light beings navigating being human. Kaku proposed that one day, physics and AI technology may be able to send us on a laser beam into another dimension or planet (Big Think, 2014). My thought is that perhaps we already do this as cosmic beings exploring the universe.

Kaku also proposed that we may need to have our consciousness stored in a computer for this to be a possibility. In addition, we would need to uncover the secret that Walter Russell inroduces centripetal and centrifugal forces, and the interaction of our energy consciousness and soul with the material world (Russell & Russell, 1926). Herein lies the greater mystery behind the infinite intelligent and loving universe we refer to as God.

In his book *The God Equation*, Kaku (2022) uses physics to guide his reader into understanding these seemingly impossible yet plausible futuristic ideas. The infinite intelligent universe inspires us through the creative minds and talent of a myriad of artists producing movies, music, scientific discoveries, and more. The evolution of consciousness is expanding beyond the limitations of the human mind to include the rapid development of AI technology. With each major paradigm shift in the arts, science, and technology, humanity awakens a new level of consciousness.

We are on the precipice of rediscovering the true source of our being, which poses many ethical questions for humanity. This paradigm shift and rediscovery have major implications for the evolution of humanity. Take, for instance, the surge in the number of productions that explore the multiverse as our collective consciousness grows into understanding the idea better. We've had movies like *Doctor Strange and the Multiverse of Madness* on traveling through time to different multiverses, *Loki* seasons one and two, *Into the Spider-Verse* and *Across the Spider-Verse* as two of the most recent Spider-Man movies, and individual productions like *Everything Everywhere All at Once*. Our culture is also flooded with ancient creation stories and tales that explore the realms of consciousness, from Star Wars to newer Japanese anime and other movies. These stories all serve as guides that help us grapple with these ideas that we do not yet fully understand.

Now, I want you to imagine that you are the boy in the above story, having lived your life unaware of the royal blood that runs through your veins or the great wealth and power that you possess. Imagine if you had never met the King or Queen and instead lived the rest of your life as a pauper. You might not have to imagine it, because many of us already live our lives like this. So many people are unaware of the great inheritance that comes from their ancestors through their DNA—the light within them that connects to the infinite universe and their divine eternal nature.

You could live outside of your inheritance as light that has no end, or you could embrace who you are and connect to higher levels of consciousness. In this chapter, we will explore this divine inheritance. As stated above, you are part of the great transmigration of souls coming and going from our planet, as seen by the great scientist and mathematician Pythagoras (Luchte, 2009). But what does that mean?

Well, souls never die, but always move from one abode and pass to another. All things change, but nothing perishes. As we've established already, no new energy can be created or destroyed; therefore, since you are energy, your essence cannot be destroyed. The soul passes hither and thither, occupying now this body, then that one; right now, yours is in the body you have currently. A great analogy is how wax can be molded into a statue and later melted down and cast differently to create a different figure, even though it is being used in the same way. So, the soul is always the same, yet it wears different forms at different times.

In the novel *Dune*, the characters wear bracelets that, if activated, create a shield around their body. The shield is represented as a glowing blue energy field that turns red whenever there is an attack. Watching this, I could not help but think about the resemblance it has to the energy fields around our bodies. While there are some differences, the representation is the same. There is a field of energy holographically within and around the body of every person, which interconnects via the chakra system and the morphogenetic resonance conducted through the human biofield.

These fields, or spheres of consciousness, vibrate at different frequencies, which informs the matrix of information stored within your DNA. According to Brennan, the human energy consciousness field (HECF), which I refer to interchangeably as the human biofield, includes the chakra system as depicted in figures 1 and 2, which is interconnected via a vertical power current. Each chakra has several vortexes that send and receive information via frequencies between the physical body and the system.

Scientists now suspect that these frequencies and fields send electrical signature impulses that activate different functions within the organs and all systems of the body. Remember, we are made of energy, and the nervous system is a complex connection that sends information in the form of electric pulses throughout the body. This system creates a unified person out of the multiplicity in your holographic form.

To understand the HECF, though, we need to take a closer look at the idea of energy fields in general, and there is no better place to start than with the father of physics, Isaac Newton. This chapter goes into the intricacies of the human energy consciousness system (HECS), exploring the four elements of our being: physical, HECF, hara dimension, and core star. It seeks to unravel the mysteries of human consciousness and its connection to the cosmic realm.

Solid Matter vs. Energy Fields

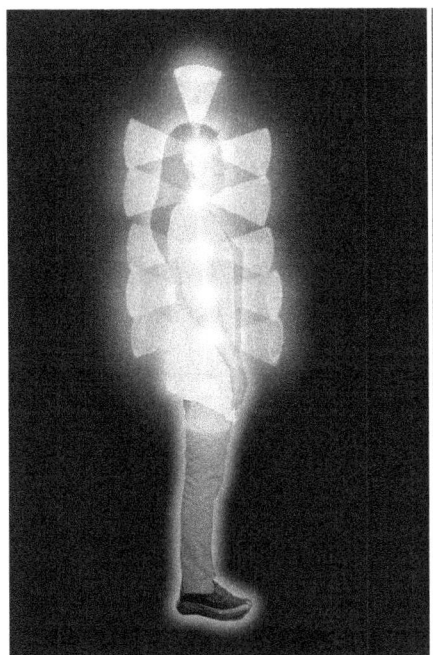 

Figure 1: HECF Side View *Figure 2: HECF Front View*

What do you see when you look at a houseplant? Well, is there anything more to it than it being a plant? The scientific answer to this used to be very simple: It is only a plant; it has mechanical processes that it performs so it stays alive as a plant, but outside of that, there is nothing more to it. The same was believed about you and me—that we are only solid matter, that we are alive inasmuch as our bodies have biological processes that keep us alive, but outside of that, there is nothing else going on.

Explanations and interpretations of natural phenomena were primarily based on tangible and observable factors. The existence of one object was believed to have no connection to how any other objects behaved until two objects physically met. Given this materialistic belief, you can see why the idea of organisms having fields of influence around them was heavily denied when it first came onto the scene. Regardless, energy fields and their impact on the universe have transformed the way we perceive and interpret various phenomena, including who we are and how we can calibrate ourselves to chase meaning.

The paradigm shift in favor of field theory began to unfold as scientific observations and experiments uncovered intricate relationships between seemingly unrelated phenomena. First, the discovery of electromagnetic fields by Faraday and Maxwell in the 19th century—as recaptured by Forbes and Mahon (2014)—marked a turning point in the recognition of energy fields as fundamental forces shaping the universe. Not only did we now believe that energy could be centered around objects, but we also believed the very Earth we live on has a huge magnetic field around it.

I love sharing phenomena that we can observe at a large scale and showing how they may explain our existence. I know when you go outside at night and look at the stars, you might think to yourself, *What splendor and beauty! How could such a vast display of brilliance ever come to exist?* Understandably so, but then you realize that the Big Bang, which gave us the universe, is mirrored in the miracle of incarnation and conception that took place in your mother's womb.

In the same way, there are striking resemblances between the Earth and the cells that make up your body. The Earth has a negative charge on the outside and a positive charge on the inside, and your cells are the same way. As Matchar (2017, para. 4) said, "Every cell in a living body contains a tiny electric charge." Think about that for a moment: The Earth is just a huge cell modeled after the cells in your body. Both your cells and the Earth are mostly neutral, but only because the positive and negative charges cancel each other out.

Science has also opened our understanding of bioelectricity—the electrical charge measured in cells, the life pulses of the body, and the electrical waves transmitted through the heart. This holographic electromagnetic field of frequencies pervades all life. Through science, we can understand that there is a magnetic and an electric charge in our cells, in the Earth, and in everything that has cells. The understanding of how energy fields interact and influence matter has provided new insights into the complexities of the natural world in ways the ancient traditions of the East had already explored hundreds of years prior.

This area of study also helps us see how the human biofield, the family field, societal fields, the educational field, and other fields are an interlocking consciousness that holographically impacts us. We are connected to other species, our environment, the Earth, and, ultimately, the universe. This knowledge has guided my life's work and become the threads that interweave my current theories of the divine genome, the divine qualities, how the infinite intelligent universe, infinite grace, and infinite divine matrices inform our human existence through the four dimensions of humankind, and the seven stages of incarnation.

I am particularly grateful to Sheldrake's morphogenetic field theory for the door it opened in the area of healing and self-discovery. The realization that we are energy and surrounded by energy brought with it the idea that we can harness that energy from the divine infinite mind and use it to bring healing to ourselves and others.

The Four Dimensions of Humankind

In 1993, Barbara Ann Brennan published her book *Light Emerging: The Journey of Personal Healing*, in which she proposes a new theory of human evolution and consciousness: the four dimensions of humankind, later renamed as the HECS (Brennan, 2011b). Her theory revolutionized and inspired my work and that of many others. This paradigm shift in thinking can also help you expand your awareness of physical, emotional, mental, relational, and spiritual health. Brennan's theory was based on years of observations using high-sense perception; by combining her experience with my own, I think we now have a comprehensive understanding of what the four dimensions are. Just as Brennan did, we will use terms like energy and dimensions in a nonscientific way and encourage researchers to explore these subtle fields—and perhaps to find new scientific terminology to describe the phenomena we have witnessed.

The more time I have spent learning and practicing these profound ideas, the more grateful I am. After 40 years of observations and teaching students how to sense and work with these subtle energy fields to promote healing, my understanding of the field of psychology, science, and healing has changed. Every experience informs and prepares me for the next, and there is no greater joy than being able to share this knowledge with others so they can grow just as I have.

Over time, and through my own experiences, I have shifted Brennan's paradigm to start with incarnation and the core star and then move down to the natural experience. From my research and teaching in energy healing, it is clear to me that we are cosmic light beings who incarnate in human form. I know how irrational all of this might sound. It did to me too, until I finally understood how the teachings of our ancient wisdom point us in this direction.

In Brennan's model, she starts with the physical body as the first dimension. This is what we experience in the materialistic models as well. Since childhood, we have learned to identify with our physical body and the material world around us first as that which is most real. The second dimension she refers to is the aura or human energy field. These are the subtle fields that directly correlate with the chakra system and with our physical, psychological, and spiritual health. In the third dimension, Brennan identifies the hara or line of intention, a dimension deeper inside that has its origin in Japanese aikido practices. The hara is the foundation for the human energy field, and it also correlates to our health and purpose in life. The fourth dimension she identifies as our core star, or the light within us. This is the creative, individuated divine spark that emerges from the black velvet void of the universe.

In *Core Light Healing: My Personal Journey and Advanced Healing Concepts for Creating the Life You Long to Live*, Brennan (2017) introduces us to the idea of the black velvet void and the core star as our original creative life pulse. This concept suggests that the black velvet void (singularity) is teeming with life that precedes the core star dimension, hara dimension, HECF dimension, and physical dimension. In the early 1980s and 1990s, these ideas were on the fringe, considered to be New Age theories without any scientific proof. Over the next 40 years, however, science—and in particular physics—has introduced new theories around the singularity that support these ideas.

Discoveries in physics, as we have discussed, have opened our field of understanding of how the universe manifests as energy and consciousness that can be measured in the tiniest quarks and gluons, which cannot break down into smaller components. The black velvet void is the deeper core star dimension and the source of all that we see and create in this world. It is there that everything comes into being, just as, out of darkness and chaos, the universe emerged and, out of the darkness of the womb, you emerged. Whenever there is something we need to manifest into being, it will come from the depths of the core star dimension, the black velvet void, the source of unlimited creative and productive power.

So, let's shift our awareness to the indivisible cosmic beginnings inherent within every cell and dimension of our beingness. We are cosmic beings made from stardust and the will of the infinite intelligence, and we emerge into this world as informational frequencies throughout the universe. Our bodies are receptors that receive those frequencies and project them into the world in which we exist. The light and energy that make up who we are manifest out of the black velvet void or singularity and come to life through the process of incarnation.

You can think of the black velvet void as the center that projects the hologram, with all the information that then makes up everything we see. All that exists in every dimension or multiverse emerges from the imagination and co-creativity of the Absolute in communion. On the next page in Figure 3, I reverse the order of the four dimensions of human kind to start with the core star.

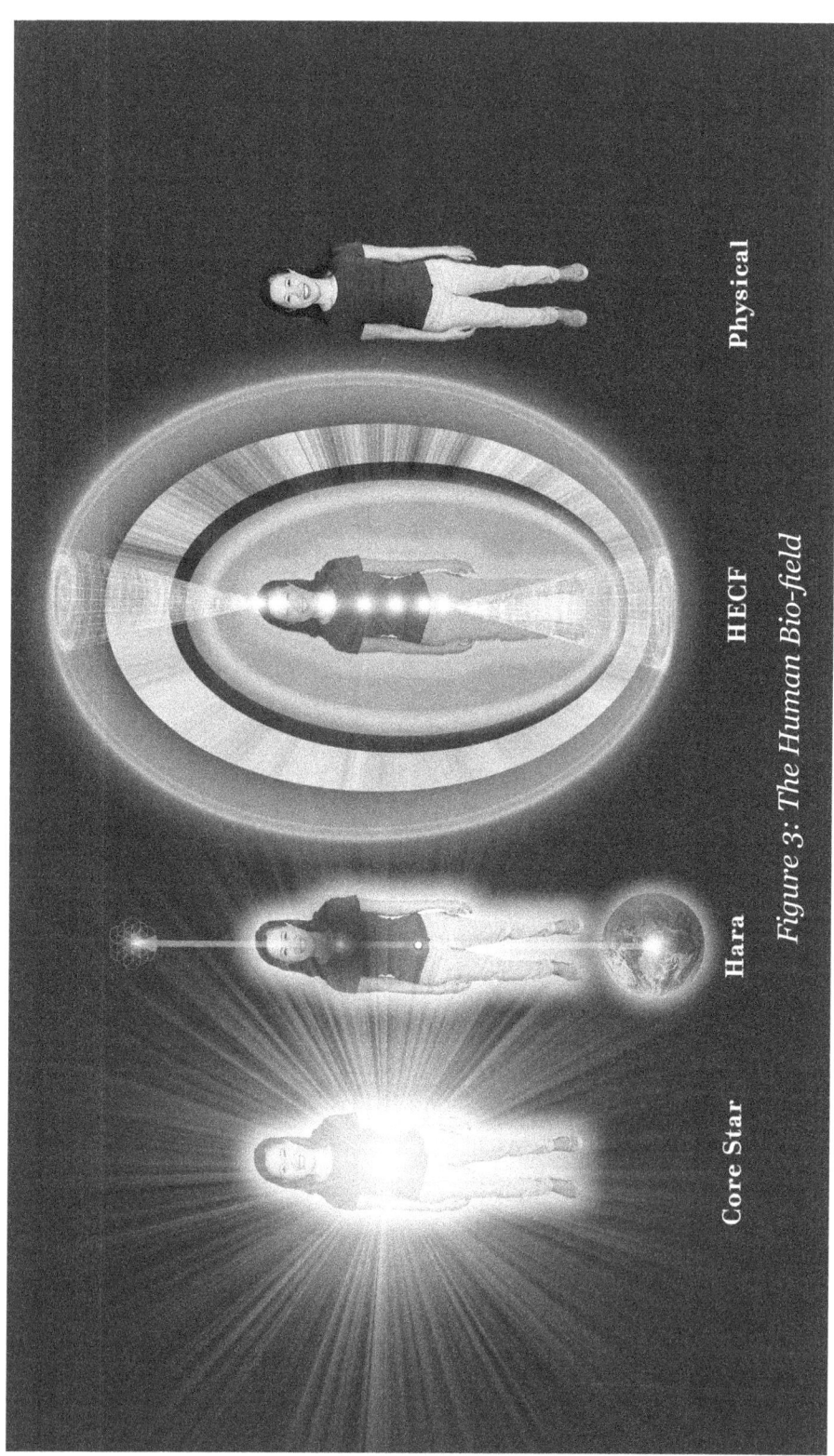

Figure 3: The Human Bio-field

The Core Star Dimension

This first dimension shows our pure form—what we were before we incarnated into the life we are living now. In the Bible, there is a running idea that we were created in the image of God and that, when we die, our souls go back to God.

The Bible says the flesh will go back into the ground where it came from and the spirit will return to God where it came from (*Holy Bible, New International Version*, 2013/1973, Ecclesiastes 3:20). I think the wording used here is phenomenal: We will "return," implying that we had an existence with God before we came to this Earth. This explains so many things in the Bible, like how God says to Jeremiah, "Before I formed you in your mother's womb, I knew you" (*Holy Bible, New International Version*, 2013/1973, Jeremiah 1:5). This is because before any of us came to be, we were all connected to the infinite Divine and existed as one with the Divine.

When our physical bodies pass on, our souls go back to becoming one with the source of light. This is our core light state, when all we are is light and we exist as one with the infinite universe, where there is oneness of mind, oneness of intention, and oneness of being with each other and with the divine mind.

The Hara Dimension

The hara dimension is the core star energy—a laser line of light that appears before the human biofield or physical body. It emerges from your core essence and appears in another dimension as your cosmic light's intention to incarnate. It is our direct connection with the cosmos and carries our intention to incarnate here on Earth. It's as if there was a spaceship above the Earth that sent down a beam so the inhabitants of the ship could be transported down through it. This is the first connection we have with the earthly realm, and it remains there throughout our lives.

This idea has been perfectly captured in the iconic statement by Descartes (2008/1637): "I think, therefore I am." This was a conclusion Descartes came to after thinking about the nature of being and questioning existence itself. The question is, how do you know you are real? How do you know anything is real? While you cannot tell for certain if everything else is real, you know that you are—because if you were not, you would not be able to ask those questions to begin with.

The hara appears two dimensions deeper than the physical body down the center of the body, connecting us to both Heaven and the Earth. Along this line, there are three points: the tan tien, the soul seat, and the ID point. There are multiple interpretations of this from different cultures, and one interesting tradition that uses this knowledge is martial arts from the East. If you watch karate and other martial arts experts as they duel or practice, you will realize they keep their hands close to the center of their bodies with their palms pointing upward. I always used to think this was a matter of fighting technique, until I noticed the pattern in so many other places.

For instance, consider the poses monks take when they are meditating or practicing aikido in Japan. Oftentimes, the participants will have their hands in a similar position but with greater symmetry. This also extends to Christianity, where having your hands in the same position is the symbol of prayer. I believe it's no coincidence that all these religions and different cultures assume this pose when they are trying to access their innermost essence or communicate with the infinite universe. I believe it is because the hara line leads back to Heaven, or the Source.

If you just place your hands in that centralized position, you instantly feel a sense of calm and peace. You can try it now. Take a deep breath and bring your palms together in front of your chest in the prayer position. How do you feel? Did your muscles release some of their tension? I bet you feel calmer and more centered. The reason for this is that your hands represent you and what you do. They are your actions and show you reaching out into the world. But when you bring them back, you are bringing yourself back into alignment with your center. Next time you are in a yoga session, check what hand positions are most common for the majority of the poses, and you will find something similar in the different positions along the hara line.

Tan Tien

The one note that keeps you incarnated here on Earth, the tan tien, is located two inches below your navel. The term Tan Tien is used in Eastern philosophy and martial arts, particularly in disciplines like tai chi and qigong, which refer to the body's center of gravity. This is often located in the lower abdomen or the area just below the navel and is considered to be a center of energy and balance. It constantly extends a strong frequency of light into the Earth, and it is through this process that we find ourselves here. Before we incarnate, the hara, through the tan tien dimension, engages with the Earth, and the interaction of the light pulse with the Earth starts the incarnation process. From dust, we are born.

The HECF or human biofield emerges out of the holographic matrix of the Earth, and our essence emerges as part of that process to bring our bodies to the experience of life on Earth. We will speak about this in more depth later in the book. Essentially, the hara is there to help us to connect to the Earth, ourselves, and Heaven. If you are connected to the Earth, you can bring the intentions of the Divine to Earth more effectively, and this also helps to ground your physical body in the natural world.

Soul Seat

The soul seat is around the center of your chest, specifically the area around the heart chakra. When you say you want something with all your heart, it's the soul seat that you are referring to. Like I said before, everything that sounds figurative is just a reality that we do not yet fully understand—in this case, a higher dimension. Your soul seat is the source of your desire and your purpose.

If you think about it, we never consider our purpose or desire as a logical consequence, but rather see it as an inspiration from somewhere that "sits in our heart"—hence the "soul seat." This is where the purpose and meaning of your life are deposited from the infinite Divine. When your soul came to Earth, it came with a set of tasks and desires and a sure purpose to be achieved during your time on this planet.

Imagine you're on an airplane about to be deployed on a mission.

You receive a device with all the information you need to fulfill your mission successfully. When you jump out of the plane and land on Earth, you will need to keep referring to that device to know what the mission is and stay on track; if you do not do this, you will end up lost in the world.

Well, right now so many people are lost in the world; they remain lost their whole lives, because they are not in touch with their soul seat, the core light that carries their mission for this life. You could also be in this space, lost and unsure of what you should be doing. Do not let that stop you from discovering your divinity, though. You are consciousness expressed in a physical body, and you have a purpose to fulfill while you are in that body.

The human condition can corrupt your desires. We talked earlier about the seven realms of consciousness that can affect your desire and purpose, the ones that map onto the seven deadly sins. When wrath, sloth, and all those other realms of consciousness take over, they draw us further and further from the true purpose that has been deposited into our lives by the infinite universe.

In addition to being the host of your intentions, purpose, and desire, the soul seat is where you process emotions related to love, grief, joy, and vulnerability. It's the place where you feel both your own emotions and the emotions of others. When you focus on your soul seat, you cultivate universal love, relational love, and self-love. Compassion, grace, and forgiveness emerge like an alchemical force, changing our pain into a softer understanding of being human.

Energy moves through the four dimensions from the Divine to your physical body. When it gets to your hara dimension, it ignites a longing in your soul seat that becomes the driver pushing you toward what is meaningful. This is why we all have different desires and purposes in life, each of us finding our unique place and allowing us to contribute to the world for the good of everyone else around us.

Take a moment to think about this. What do you desire the most in life? If time and money were not constraints, what would you spend your time doing that would make you happy? In some cases, the mind will rush to superficial pleasures when this question is asked. But go beyond that level of consciousness. Superficial pleasures will and can never make you happy; all they are is a low vibrational frequency that our human condition resorts to when we fail to remain in connection with the divine infinite universe.

So, what do you want in life? If everything went your way, what would you want your legacy to be? If you search your soul seat, your heart, you will find the answer to all these questions, which will help you find the motivation and energy to pursue what is meaningful—that which comes from Heaven itself—rather than what is expedient.

The Human Energy Consciousness Field

The HECF or the human biofield is the source feeding into the physical body and giving it the energy and instruction that come from the higher dimensions. I love thinking of the human biofield as the transportation dimension, controlling the flow of information from your divine essence to your physical dimension and also processing the information your physical body encounters.

Think about the relationship between the Moon and the Sun for a moment. The Moon is always being drawn to Earth because of the Earth's gravitational pull. At the same time, the force around the Moon influences tides and weather patterns here on Earth. The two huge masses do not interact physically at all. Regardless of this, though, they still affect each other significantly.

The reason there is still a correlation between the Moon and the Earth despite them not having a physical connection is that they both have a field of energy around them that guides their movement. This is how our bodies are as well—the action in our biofield will have an impact on how our physical bodies work and how they interact with the world around us. The anatomy of our energy field projects holographically through our physical bodies and interpenetrates them to align with our joints, organs, and major endocrine glands. While you cannot see your energy field, you can feel it. You probably feel it every day as you interact with different people.

Think of a situation where you are sitting on a bench in the park on a nice sunny day. You are happy watching joggers and dog walkers pass by as you read your favorite book. Now imagine someone walks over to you and stands right in front of you, such that if they moved any further, their shoes would touch yours. Let's say they are dressed very well, look good, and smell amazing. They even have a big smile across their face and seem friendly.

How would you feel, though? One moment you are alone, and the next moment a stranger is standing right in front of you, with no space between you at all. I bet you would lean back and feel uncomfortable. Even though nothing is threatening or repulsive about their physical appearance, you would still move back and feel unease. Why is that? If all there is to both you and them are your physical bodies, then shouldn't you feel like they are being intrusive only if they physically touch you or if they smell or look bad?

No, because even though physically everything looks separated, just like the Moon and the Earth, the higher dimensions of your beings are touching and interacting. This is why you would say something like, "You are intruding on my space." You have a space around and within you that influences how you feel and, eventually, act. This is the control center for your emotions as well, helping you manage and understand the nonphysical parts of your being.

Here is a simple exercise to notice how you experience different people's energy already in your everyday life. Like I said before, figures of speech are normally not just figures of speech. Think about how you would say someone's energy was "off," or how we refer to smiles and joy with words like "bright" and "shining." Everyone does this, even when they do not believe there is a literal representation of these phrases at a higher dimension in the person they are referring to.

Our very language is shaped in a way that acknowledges the existence of a biofield that is presented in colorful energy. Even now, you can probably think of some friends, family members, or colleagues who are fun to be around and raise your spirits; on the other hand, other people bring you down or make you feel anxious. These experiences are being transmitted and received by your interactive biofield in the same way that your bodies and minds are exchanging information naturally.

There is an interesting read by Rupert Sheldrake (2011), *Dogs That Know When Their Owners Are Coming Home: And Other Unexplained Powers of Animals*, that I find interesting. In the book, he shares how there are so many documented cases of pet owners who have noticed that their pets know when they are coming home. These pets can tell who is at the door even when they are upstairs and too far away to pick out a scent.

There is an energy field around your body that informs even your physical senses in a way that you might not understand. Consider the following questions:

- Have you ever felt like someone was looking at you, and then you turned to see someone behind you?

- Have you ever felt like someone you loved was in trouble, and then you found out something bad had happened to them?

- Have you ever thought, completely out of the blue, of someone you haven't spoken to for a while, and then you meet them that same week or they call you?

- Have you ever felt like you were about to receive a call, and when you look at your phone, it rings?

Most people have experienced at least two of these scenarios, and there are so many more phenomena just like these in our daily lives. I know we hardly ever stop and ask ourselves why being looked at would feel a certain way—nothing in the natural world's science supports these ideas. But when you consider the biofield, all these things start to make sense.

Experiencing the Human Biofield

With high perception, you can feel and interact with the human biofield through your physical senses—for example, by sensing the energy around others physically through your hands. If you try to do this with a friend, you might be able to feel the human biofield. Here is what I want you to do: Go outside to a park or garden if you can. Close your eyes and sense the energy around the plants in front of you. Notice how different plants make you feel and how their structure and shape contribute to that feeling.

Don't stop there, but be conscious of this field everywhere you go. Notice how you feel walking into a room with total strangers or in the hustle and bustle at the airport versus the calm of the beach. When you are in a line and everyone else there is impatient and grumpy, how does that make you feel? In contrast, what about when you see kids running around a playground—how does that make you feel?

Notice the subtleties. Notice the sound of someone's voice—how does the pitch or tone impact you? These are all vibrational frequencies that interact directly with your biofield. Can you sense the energy of someone pushy or someone who feels like they drain your energy? Or perhaps a person who talks over a group or withdraws from everyone else? How does that energy feel in your body? What arises in you?

Ask yourself, how is your nervous system picking up signals from the invisible energy in the biofield and converting them into the feelings that you have? There must be something else that helps with this process—a part of you that interacts with the energy and translates it to your physical perceptions.

The human biofield has seven layers corresponding with the physical dimension. These layers are distributed through the chakra system, an ancient Eastern philosophy that conceptualizes the energy vortexes that are holographically projected through us. We'll explore the fundamental ideas of the chakra system in the next chapter to better understand the human biofield around each of us.

The Physical Dimension

We have already established that everything we see and interact with physically is made up of energy. The Big Bang, the breath from which everything we know was created, was an explosion of energy into matter and antimatter. The yin and yang of light and dark matter then spun out to create our beautiful cosmos. In the same way, our physical bodies are the final representation of the explosion of light from the infinite universe.

Your physical body is the expression of your essence that is furthest from your true nature as light. It is projected and created through the interaction between the DNA from your parents and the centripetal and centrifugal forces that take action when the egg and the sperm meet.

The physical dimension is like a shell that we need to experience the life the natural world has to offer. We are privileged to come to this world and reincarnate our essence into a finite body. This is the true miracle: that we can express ourselves in the physical body that we are in now. I want you to take a minute and think about the reality of your physical body, how unique it is, and how special it is to house your essence. So many complex processes and organs are working to keep your body up and healthy, and all of the functionality has come down directly from the human energy field, which I refer to as the human biofield. Our physical bodies are made of energy, and if we move up to the next dimension, we can see what the field of energy around our bodies looks like.

This chapter was an overview of the four dimensions of your existence. In the next chapter, we will follow how you came from being pure light to manifest in this world in seven stages. Some of these stages are based on the four dimensions to illustrate your divine origins.

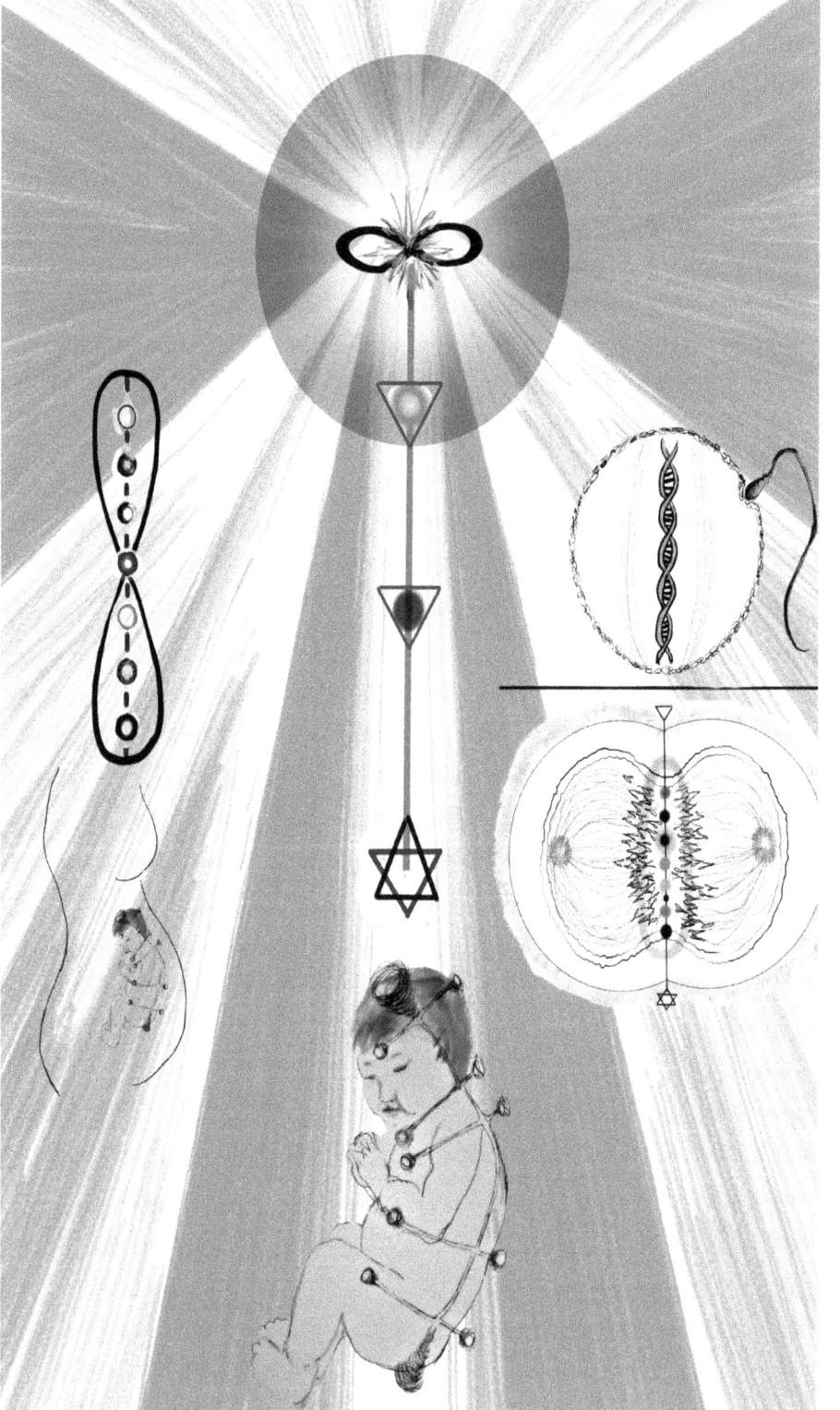

Chapter 4:

The Seven Stages of Incarnation

The more you understand the greatness that is within you and your true nature as a descendant of the divine mind, the closer you come to unraveling your divine genogram. Focusing on the phenomenology that transcends your body is by no means an attempt to downplay your body's importance to life—far from it. Your body is the vessel through which you can experience consciousness, as you are doing now. It's your physical body that receives information from the divine mind through your energy field and then translates that information into the world.

We are light. When we look at the model proposed by Brennan, this light is the core star we discussed in the previous chapter. But how does this light incarnate into who you are today? How is that information and energy transferred from higher dimensions and incarnated to allow you to have your human experience here?

The miracle of life is a journey more than it is a moment of spontaneous combustion. You are a carefully crafted being, and it took time and very complex processes for you to be created. You can never reduce your existence to the biological processes that created you. You are far more than that—you are light voyaging across the galaxy, and you have found a home in your current form for a temporary time only.

Your energy can never die or end, though, so after this life you will exist only as the core light, until you find your way through the hara into another life form here on Earth. Brennan's chakra system helps us identify the manifestation process, which emerges from the double torus or Flower of Life. The paired opposites in the vortexes ignite with the electrical charge and complex wave frequencies that interact with each other and inform the DNA during our inception.

In the previous chapter, we went over the four dimensions of your existence, which are all simultaneously a part of you. In this chapter, however, we will explore in depth the process through which you move from being pure light to incarnate in the Earth's holographic matrix. This is the miracle: We manifest from nothing, first appearing like a caterpillar, then becoming a human being. Our chakra system is constantly sending frequencies to every organ of the body, from our inception until we are fully formed. The cells do not know what they should form into, but the vortexes in a chakra have frequencies that turn on to guide the process.

The seven stages that we are going to walk through are: the core star or the divine spark; the hara; the double torus (the chakras and the human biofield, and the sperm and the egg); cells dividing; the mother with zygote in utero; the mother with fetus; and, lastly, the neonate or baby.

Brennan developed these ideas in *Light Emerging* (Brennan, 2011b), and many people were inspired by her work. Dr. Wayne Dyer's inspirational book *The Power of Intention* is one example, and it was a *New York Times* bestseller. In a private conversation with Brennan, Dyer mentioned that the section on hara in *Light Emerging* impacted his life deeply, as at the time he was in deep self-reflection about the dynamics of his family. It seemed as if his marriage and life were dissolving around him, but that chapter was an inspiration and helped him through one of the darkest

Figure 4: The Seven Stages of Incarnation

moments in his life.

Just as we highlighted earlier, the chakras are like an electrical information transporting system turning on, just like your computer turns on a program. They are turning on the divine plan in the DNA for your kidneys, your stomach, your heart, your brain, and everything else. We are vibration, we are frequency; if the body does not have that electrical charge from the light, it cannot be alive.

The chakras and vortices transmit billions of vibrational frequencies that inform our bodies' functioning, from cellular awareness to all systems and organs. There is very little known about the interaction between the core essence, hara, and the transmission of light through the chakra system, but acupuncture and ancient Hindu teachings give us some direction toward researching the complexities of these interactive systems. It's as if the human body is one of the most sophisticated bio-organisms.

Stage One
Core Star

According to Brennan and the other scientific theories we explored in the previous chapter, your core star was created in the first stage. This is also referred to as the Big Bang, Big Breath, or, in Jewish texts, "let there be light." All creation stories signify that at the beginning, light was formed out of the black velvet void; there was light, and all existence is part of the intricate holographic web of infinite intelligence that comes from that light.

We call this light God! We are made in the image and likeness of this light. We are a divine spark that holographically is a fractal of the whole. Christ's words, "I and the Father are One" (*Holy Bible, New International Version*, 2013/1973, John 10:30), guide us toward remembering this truth. This passage is gravely misunderstood, though. Christ is saying, "I am the Christ Light; I came before you in the great expansion. I am the Son; you are His children." We have come from the light.

Here is the greatest mystery, which was even hidden in the

Figure 5: The Core Star

Garden of Eden, where Adam and Eve—who were in light form and hadn't fully incarnated into human form—activated the Kundalini, the serpent at the base of the spine. This life force, left untamed, is renamed by Freud as the id, the unbridled life force that is tamed or mediated by our human ego. It is interesting that in all these stories we find light, life force, and electricity. Wilhelm Reich, a student of Freud's, veered off to call this force the libido or creative life force, then orgone energy. You can see how excited I get connecting and interweaving these beautiful creation stories—there is no end to the connections and lessons buried beneath them.

So, we emerge as an individuated light, a cosmic being, from the black velvet void. Our journey and incarnation here occur when, from our core, we interpenetrate another dimension (Brennan calls this the hara dimension), then create a human biofield, which becomes the foundation for our physical human experience. Let's look at the next stage of incarnation.

Stage Two
Hara Dimension

In the second stage of incarnation, as shown in Figure 6, you will notice the core light penetrating into the hara dimension and see the infinity sign. This is where the Flower of Life interpenetrates this dimension and sends a direct beam of light, hara, or line of intention to the Earth. At the Individuation Point is the incarnation point where as an individuated divine spark of infinite intelligence, infinite grace and love, and infinite probabilities for incarnating into the earthplane begin.

The next unfoldment at this stage is the soul seat or seed pod of divinity that is a holographic matrix of the cosmos that includes the soul's intentions. The light at the soul seat is another Flower of Life frequency that expresses the soul's longing and purpose for incarnating on Earth.

The third aspect is referred to as the Tan Tien, according to Brennan In *Light Emerging*, it becomes the one note that

Figure 6: The Hara Dimension

anchors the soul on Earth. I prefer to reference it as a quantum concentrated conscious life force that anchors the incoming soul's core presence and intentions. It forms an energetic matrix with the power to interpenetrate the morphogenetic field of the Earth and pass through all of the astral realms and energetic noise bands and frequencies that embody the earth planes memory field. All sentient life on earth, has a holographic matrix that represents its form prior to materialization.

Stage Three
Development of the Double Torus

In the third stage of incarnation, you can see the Flower of Life emerging from infinity. After engaging through the hara with the Earth, it appears as the double torus, which is the foundational human biofield where the chakras and vertical power current appear. Recent research on the bioelectricity of the body indicates that the source of this electrical information and frequencies may directly relate to the chakra system (Rastogi et al., 2021).

You might now be wondering how this electrical current informs, regulates, and transmits consciousness throughout the matrix of our body. Well, scientists are recognizing that this invisible electrical field directly correlates to the health and functioning of all bodily systems.

Entering the Earth plane involves coming into the astral field around the Earth, as shown in Figure 7a. This is the bridge between the heavenly and earthly realms and a part of the Akashic field or A-field. If you look from the top to the bottom, you will see the following:

1. The seventh chakra relates to the seventh level of the human biofield and is a holographic structured energy, image, or fractal of the infinite intelligence arising from the core through the chakra system. The divine mind is related to the divine wisdom that informs us.

2. The sixth chakra is related to divine love and ecstasy. The transmission of infinite grace and transfigurative love

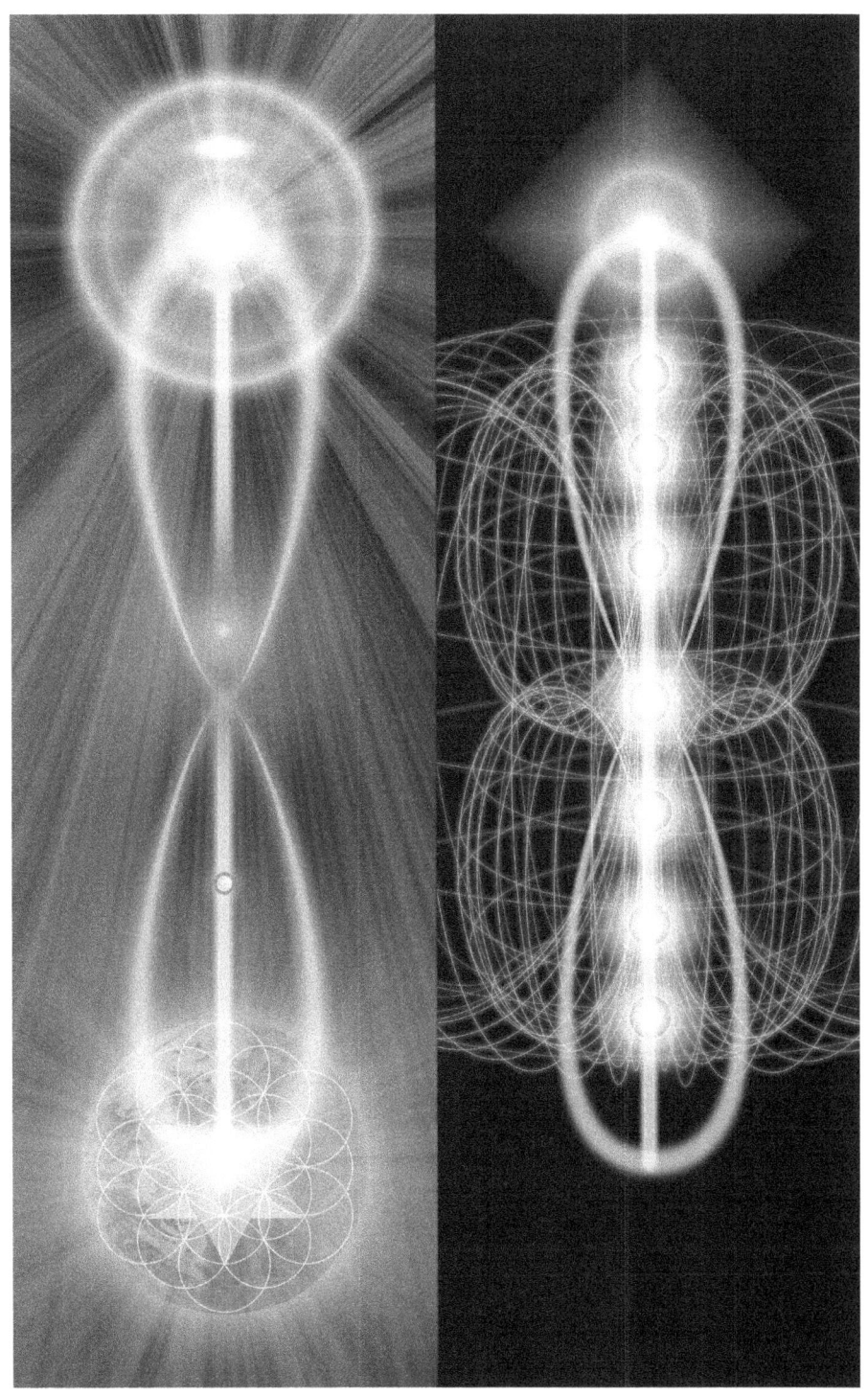

Figure 7a: Double Torus   *Figure 7b: Chakras*

emerges through this chakra and level. It connects directly via the vertical power current with the seventh chakra. This also activates the brain's pineal gland, which stimulates our visual cortex and gives us a higher spiritual experience.

3. The fifth chakra correlates to the fifth level of the field and is a direct imprint of the divine matrix of the universe interacting with the Earth plane. According to Brennan, the fifth-level holographic matrix is like a human biochip that includes all the coding of the universe, the Earth, and the human body. It is the matrix that informs the DNA of human cells and is essential in creating the first level of the human biofield. On a higher frequency note, in its very nature, it is divine will. On the lower level of the field, it correlates to divine communication, or how we hear and speak from our higher-level consciousness.

4. The fourth chakra and fourth level is the bridge, as we mentioned before. We are impacted by this level when moving into a relationship with the Earth plane. During incarnation, we enter the different spheres of consciousness around the Earth, an astral field with many different realms. It includes all of Earth's history, which is stored in the A-field, and as we travel through these realms, we take on certain ideas and modes from the history of the world.

   Some of the main challenging modes, to the right side of the double torus, are the levels of consciousness we will encounter and need to master on Earth. Many traditions have spoken about them, such as the Jewish texts, which call them "the seven sins." At the same time, you will be entering your country, your social, cultural, and religious traditions, and your family field. The information is all communicated through the fourth chakra and goes into building your holographic representation.

   This chakra and level stores all of our memories of human relationships and opens us to divine human love and free will. Through the seals of the fourth chakra, there is a direct transmission of infinite grace and love coming from the core, descending from the sixth level as divine love; then the frequency changes as it enters the Earth plane of human relational love. The love is being transmitted from the core, yet the frequency changes as it enters through the chakra system.

This will all become clearer in Chapter eight when we discuss the divine qualities and how to use them for healing and building your life. When we enter the lower half of the double torus, all of these chakras are undeveloped and become imprinted by the positive and negative experiences we have on Earth.

5. On the lower half of the double torus is the third chakra. The third chakra and third level relate to the divine human mind and are a holographic image of the seventh chakra and seventh level, the divine mind. The third chakra and level accumulate and record all of your memories, life experiences, educational experiences, blessings, and traumas. It is a record of all your healthy and unhealthy belief systems, and it relates to both your positive and negative love bonds with others.

   This chakra develops in early childhood through each experience, from sitting up to crawling, talking, and learning. It is our center, where we develop a sense of belonging and figure out who we are. It is here where we learn divine respect. We can feel our center and respond from who we are rather than from what others tell us about who we are. It is here where we also record all the impressions from the outer world that can lead us astray and induce self-doubt.

6. The second chakra and second level correlate to how we feel about ourselves, as well as to the core transmission of infinite grace and love. The infinite grace subsides into the sixth level as divine love, then the frequency changes into human love on the fourth level, and then on the second level translates to self-love and self-acceptance.

   There is only one love that is transmitted, but its frequency changes as it moves through the seals of the chakras and becomes clouded by our human experiences. In some areas of our lives, love flows freely, while in other areas—where we hold on to pain, anger, grief, or trauma—love becomes bonded until we unravel the entanglement. We will discuss the process of unraveling these areas in a later chapter.

7. The first chakra and first level relate to our will to live and our ability to trust in the world. This chakra and level are a direct imprint from the fifth level and hold the matrix for the physical body. When we experience different types of trauma, whether physical, emotional, mental, relational, or spiritual, our ability to trust is disrupted. The divine quality that relates to this chakra is divine trust. This is also the chakra and level where we want to align our will to bring coherence into our field.

The Rats That Changed Morphogenetics

In the book *A New Science of Life* (Sheldrake, 1995), one chapter goes over experiments on rats that proved the morphogenetic field exists. At the time of these experiments, family systems—which we will cover in Chapter six—had already started to take shape. William McDougall, who understood the idea of family systems, set out in 1920 to prove that if rats learned a new skill, then the next generation, which shared the same DNA through familial relations, would learn the same skill faster.

To show this, he set up an experiment where rats would navigate a maze with multiple options. One of the paths was well-lit while the other was not, and every time the rat came out through the well-lit path, it would be given an electric shock. He then took rats that had been bred from the original rats in the experiment to make sure they shared some DNA and gene similarities, and had them go through the maze.

The idea was to test how many rounds it would take until a rat stopped going through the well-lit exit. The first generation of rats would need to be shocked several times before they began to hesitate to take the well-lit path. Eventually, they would stop taking the well-lit path altogether, with very few exceptions. Over 15 years, McDougall would experiment on about 32 generations of rats, and the results were phenomenal: The first generation took an average of over 200 tries to learn the maze compared to under

30 tries for the 32nd generation. The graph produced of these results over the years shows a very clear and consistent decrease, demonstrating that rats that are related transmit information such as learning to the next generation.

While this was impressive, it was hardly revolutionary. Family systems had already established these correlations, and they could be noticed in human families as well. What happened later on, when the experiment was repeated with the addition of a control group, is what changed everything.

See, in the first experiment, there were no tests done on the rats whose parents had never received any electronic shock training to make sure the results were definitive. In the new experiment, the scientists found that all the rats started learning much faster than in the previous experiment. This was shocking, because the rats in the two groups were neither related nor in the same location. However, the morphogenetic field affected how all the rats learned this trick. So, the only way to change the results was to teach the rats a new skill altogether. When the rats were tested with a new task, the results were consistent: Subsequent generations all learned the skill faster than the previous ones, despite the control group not having been trained.

Does this mean there is a field that shares information within species that is not governed by the natural channels of information sharing? I will leave you to think about that. In my observation, morphic resonance proves that morphogenetic fields evolve and are inherited through nonlocal resonance, allowing for the transmission of collective memories and behaviors within species. This implies that new behaviors can spread rapidly within a species, facilitating learning and adaptation.

Moreover, morphogenetics extends beyond biological organisms to encompass social groups and human societies, shaping collective memories and behaviors transmitted through cultural rituals and traditions. This highlights the pervasive nature of morphic fields in shaping various aspects of life.

In the same way that we challenged the materialistic view of the world, let's also challenge the conventional notion of fixed and eternal natural laws and consider the possibility of morphic resonance as an evolutionary view, where these laws evolve along with nature itself. This evolutionary approach is based on nonlocal similarity reinforcement, illustrating how patterns of activity in self-organizing systems are influenced by past patterns through morphic resonance.

This theory also extends to mental activity, perceptions, and telepathy, suggesting that morphic fields underlie human consciousness and communication. There is evidence supporting telepathic abilities in both animals and humans. These are ideas that I explore further in another of my books, *The Mysteries of ESP, the Cosmos, and the Universe*.

Stage Four
Cell Division

In the fourth stage of incarnation, we select our mother and father, joining with the sperm and egg during cellular division. We select the region, culture, and family of origin in which we will incarnate before entering into the womb of our mothers or connecting with them during in vitro fertilization (IVF), and this is expressed through conception.

Upon entering the womb of our mother, or beforehand in the case of IVF, we blend with the cellular division process, selecting DNA coding and emotional coloring from both our maternal and paternal families of origin. When we have chosen the place and family we will be born into, the transfer of information from the chakra system to the cells then begins. Epigenetics and morphogenetics come into play and start interacting with the DNA to create you. The chakra system, which consists of sets of two opposing chakras, informs cellular division via energy impulses. Walter Russell introduced the idea of the fulcrum between two vortexes as an interdimensional gateway between the core realms of consciousness and the Earth plane. Tesla said about Walter Russell: "Walter's writing on cosmogony should be hidden for 1,000 years until humanity is ready for it" (Paul, 2022). We will explore his ideas in more detail in the next chapter.

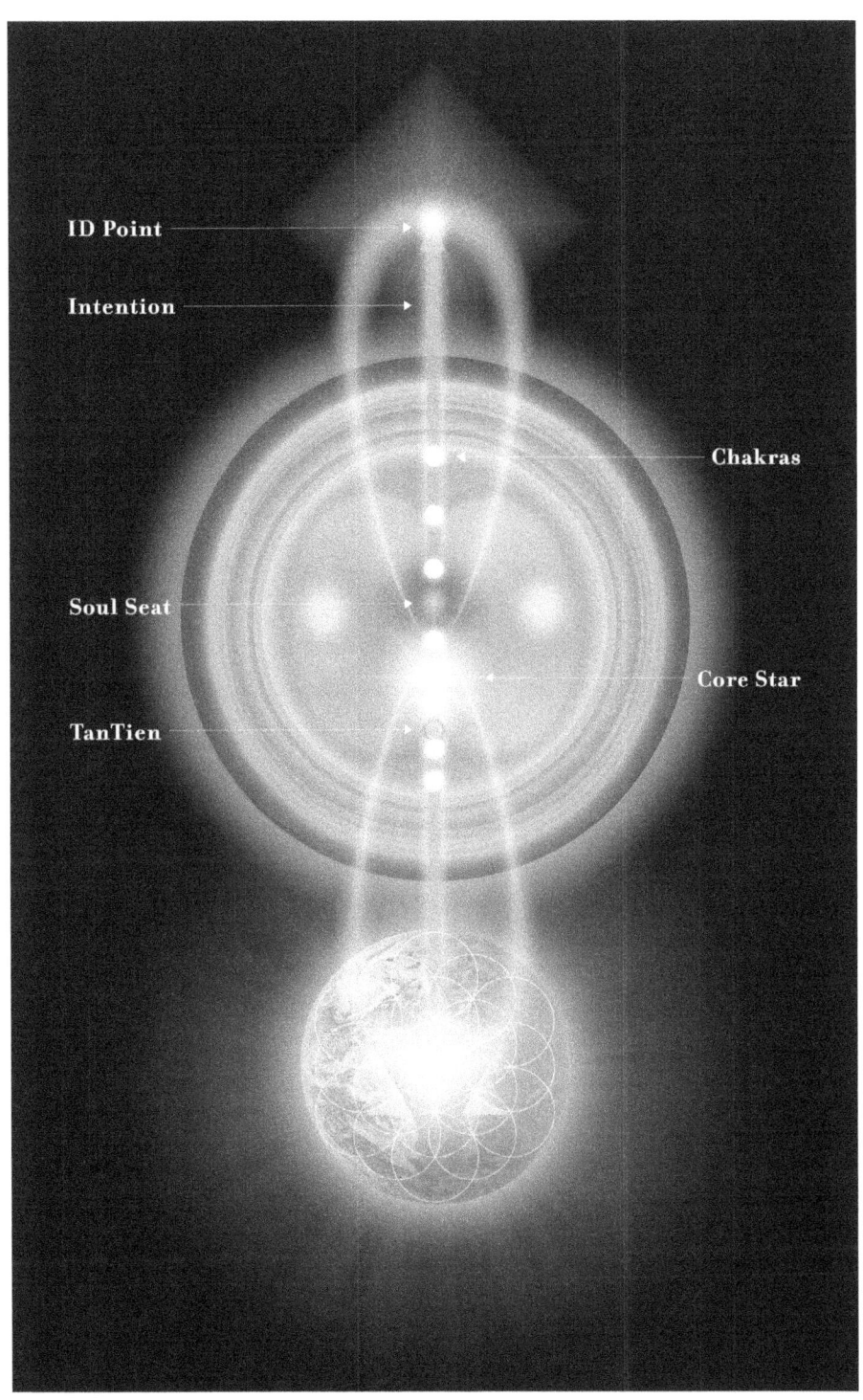

Figure 8: Cell Division

Your energy enters the womb and connects with the sperm and then the egg through that cosmic explosion. As it was at the start of time, so it is in the womb—the black velvet void of the universe.

All of a sudden, the sperm and the egg start replicating, just like the universe does. We are replicating the universe, which is why we have a right side and a left side. Walter Russell talks about everything being in polarity, like yin and yang. As soon as you hit the gravitational and radiation pool on Earth, there's always that polarity as the double torus appears—as the infinity sign and the Flower of Life.

As shown in Figure 8, the hara line and the chakra are already there when the cell starts dividing. They are informing the cell through electrical impulses and frequencies, an intricate part of cellular division. The cells continue to replicate and inform the divine design of a human zygote, the next stage.

Stage Five
Zygote

In Figure 9, we can see a fetus growing following the morphogenetic field that expresses the divine design of a human being. The development of the zygote is a complex process that takes into consideration not only the DNA but also the morphogenetic field of a human being.

This is also the template that we saw at the fifth level, which is the divine outline of the human body. At this stage, the human body starts to form, following the infinite intelligent information transmitted via the human biofield and the DNA present within the fertilized egg. When you enter and engage with the Earth plane during the hara stage, you activate the human biofield and chakras; that is, you intend to incarnate as a human rather than as an elephant or a walrus.

Within the hologram of the Earth is every field of life—all those frequencies that make a rose a rose, a tree a tree, and a human a human. These fields are integrated into the hologram, and we will refer to them as morphogenetic fields as other scientists

Figure 9: Zygote

like Russell and Sheldrake have done. The energetic form of a human body starts to appear around the hara, drawing from the morphogenetic structure that is already stored in the memory field of the Earth. The morphogenetic field is what gives you your form and the essence of what it is to be human.

However, this developing form is not independent in its development, so it is connected to the mother in the uterus until later in the process.

Stage Six
Fetus in Utero

In Figure 10, the fifth stage, the fetus comes into form and is now recognizable via ultrasound technology. The DNA is activated by the energy from the chakras. All the bodily systems and organs are formed and the readiness to exit the embodiment of the mother's womb is activated. The process of moving from the unmanifest to the manifest world—the transfiguration process of incarnation from light into form, like the caterpillar to the butterfly—is almost complete, and you are ready to emerge from your mother's womb into the Earth plane. Our field begins to form within the already established field of our mother. Within this matrix are also all the consciousness of our father and our ancestors.

The chakras of the fetus, as shown in Figure 10, are not yet developed; they are only spots on the developing fetus. Throughout this stage, the fetus depends heavily on the mother's biofield as a holographic replica of its own. The holographic field of the mother, father, and family act as a protective shield as the infant goes through each developmental stage, until its own chakras have developed. This process of field and chakra development is a part of every developmental stage as we move toward individuation and autonomy. The energetic system becomes a memory field of all the life experiences before and after birth.

Figure 10: Fetus in Utero

Stage Seven
The Infant

When you get to this stage of incarnation, you will now have the chakras showing on the front and the back of your body, as depicted in Figure 11. However, the openings are still very small and will continue to mature during the various life cycles of your becoming an individuated human being. At this stage, the seventh chakra—the top vortex—is wider than the bottom one because you have not yet fully grounded yourself in the Earth.

From here on out, the infant starts to interact with the world and use those experiences to familiarize themself with it. Throughout this process, they are still dependent on their mother, but they are slowly moving into independence. The more the chakras develop, the more independent the infant and later child become from their parents. The biofield of the mother, father, and relatives will protect and inform the child until they eventually have their own strong biofield.

This is the end of the incarnation process, by which point your light will have arrived here on Earth. The mission from here will be to learn to share the light and blessings that you bring to the world. You were born into transgenerational patterns of both positive and negative love bonds. The negative love bonds, or unhealthy patterns, will actually awaken you to reclaim the light within. When you unravel the mystery of the entangled web, you will find the divine qualities and light that were suppressed.

Let's now explore the fascinating journey of your ancestors and yourself and discover the blessings you were designed to bring to the Earth and humanity. In the coming chapters, we will look at the family systems that hold these negative love bonds, how trauma affects the flow of your energy, and how you can bring your divine qualities to life.

Figure 11: The Infant Stage

Epigenetics

In his groundbreaking 1926 work *The Universal One*, and revisions in the 1947 book *Science of Light*, Walter Russell shaped the concept of epigenetics (Russell, 1926; Russell, 1947). Russell's concept of "the interpenetration of all things" suggested that the universe is not a collection of isolated entities but rather a vast, interconnected web. Everything, from the smallest subatomic particle to the grandest galaxy, is fundamentally linked and constantly interacts. This interpenetration can be seen as a metaphor for how the environment plays a crucial role in shaping life, but there was an insistence in Russell's work that this was more than just a metaphoric view of the world.

Moreover, he claimed that organisms do not exist in a vacuum; they are constantly bombarded with environmental cues, both physical (light, temperature) and chemical (nutrients, pollutants). These cues can influence an organism's development, behavior, and even gene expression. Imagine a single cell in a developing organism. The surrounding environment provides a constant stream of information: the presence of oxygen, the availability of nutrients, and the pressure of neighboring cells. This information, in turn, guides the cell's behavior. It might differentiate into a specific type of tissue, activate the production of certain proteins, or initiate cell division. In this way, the environment becomes an integral part of the organism's makeup, a testament to the interconnectedness Russell envisioned.

Russell further emphasized the rhythmic nature of the universe. He believed that all phenomena, from the movement of planets to the beating of our hearts, operate in cycles and rhythms. This concept finds interesting parallels in modern scientific discoveries regarding the influence of environmental rhythms on biological processes.

The day–night cycle is a fundamental environmental rhythm that has a profound impact on living organisms. Plants open their stomata to capture sunlight for photosynthesis during the day, while animals exhibit circadian rhythms in sleep–wake patterns, hormone production, and even cellular activity. These responses are not simply passive reactions; they are adaptations honed by evolution to maximize survival and fitness within the rhythmic context of the environment. Similarly, seasonal changes can trigger animal migrations, plant flowering, and even immune function variations. These examples highlight how organisms are attuned to the rhythmic nature of their environment and respond accordingly.

While Russell's ideas struggled to find recognition from the scientific world when they were first published, they offer a compelling metaphor for understanding the intricate relationship between organisms and their environment. Modern scientific research in epigenetics and ecology delves deeper into the specific mechanisms by which the environment shapes life. These ideas were later amplified by the work of Bruce Lipton, which we will also explore in this chapter. By combining these established scientific fields with the broader philosophical framework proposed by Russell, we can gain a richer understanding of the universe's interconnected symphony and the role organisms play within it.

Biology of Belief

Bruce Lipton, a cell biologist, published work on genetics that drew some powerful correlations between the mind and its influence over our biology (Lipton, 2005). Lipton argued that genes are not the sole determinants of our health and well-being but rather act in response to signals from the environment, including our belief systems. He noted that the fluid surrounding the DNA is a conduit for information that impacts both individual cells and our overall health. This places the HECS at the center of everything that happens in your biology.

His work extensively explores the ideas behind epigenetics, showing how the environment is constantly sending messages that can influence gene expression without changing your genetic code. This means there is a system around each cell and around you that responds to the energy with which you interact, therefore affecting the outcome of your life, even at a biological level.

Lipton and Bhaerman (2011) highlight research showing how external stimuli, like stress or positive affirmations, can modify the activity of your genes, suggesting that our thoughts and emotions, shaped by our environment and beliefs, can play a significant role in our health and potentially influence the development of diseases. This is important to know for everyone, especially healers. If the energy we interact with can lead to disease, then the ability to channel light back in through the chakra system can certainly bring restoration.

While genes are important, it is crucial to remember that they are just a part of who we are. They are only a result of our incarnation, and we existed long before the genes themselves came to be. The genetic code that makes up your DNA is an expression of the energy that you manifest in physical form on Earth. It's not the other way around—you are not influenced by your genes, but rather you developed them, and you can certainly influence them. As Lipton puts it, the genes are like antennae, receiving and responding to signals from the energy field. These signals, including our perception of the world, can activate or deactivate certain genes, ultimately affecting our cellular function and, potentially, our health outcomes.

Without question, our genes are only receivers of information. Your early childhood experiences program your subconscious with limiting or empowering beliefs that will have an impact on your life. However, if you have allowed trauma and negativity to block the flow of information, the potential that you had when you entered this world has not been lost. You can still discover the true potential that your divine origins grant and burden you with.

Lipton's work has been met with criticism. This is mostly because the field of epigenetics is still evolving, and the exact mechanisms by which environment and beliefs influence gene expression are not fully understood. What is certain, however, is that the idea is coherent in so many ways with the experiences I have witnessed over and over again throughout my career in teaching and practicing energy healing.

In a recent interview posted by Greaterness Coaching (2018), Lipton explained how he started to realize that it's not our genes that are the determining factor of our lives but rather the information that our genes receive. Lipton explains in this interview that while he was still working at Stanford Medical School, he would take a cell and put it in a container, and over a couple of days it would multiply rapidly—as stem cells do. He repeated this a couple of times, and every time the cells would be the same.

Eventually, however, he started to place the same cells in different containers, and there was a baffling difference. The cells changed as they multiplied, even though they were in the same place. So, these cells started to change when they were in different environments, even though their genes were the same. Well, think about how this affects you and your life. You have a set of genes, and you have cells that get their instructions from those genes. So, if you change the information that your cells and genes receive, you can change how your entire body functions. The main influences affecting the environment of your genes, however, are morphogenetic. The morphogenetic fields carry vibrational frequencies that influence not only the genes but also the structure.

Chapter 5:
Human Evolution: Essence Into Matter

James Leininger

James Leininger can meticulously recount his past life as James Huston Jr., a World War II pilot who died in a plane crash. He claims vivid memories of being a pilot and has shared specific details about his supposed previous life multiple times, with consistency between these accounts. One remarkable aspect is his recounting of the plane crash, which aligns with verified historical events he could not have known otherwise. His story has sparked immense interest and controversy around the idea of reincarnation and past lives across the scientific, religious, and psychological fields.

The case of James Leininger brought the concept of reincarnation into the spotlight, but it was already part of the conversation for many scientists and religions. One such person is Bruce Lipton, whose work we have discussed in previous chapters. The idea that our bodies are receptors for the energy that carries our essence marks his work, and it has also inspired my understanding of the incarnation process and the infinite state that our souls are in.

What makes the story of James Leininger an outlier is how undeniable it is that something other than divine connection could have been at play. James Leininger's world wasn't filled with airplanes or talk of war as he grew up; there was no direct influence to speak of. He was just two years old, full of toys and the confusion of a new life. Then, the terrors began—nightmares, vivid and terrifying, of fire, loud noises, and a feeling of falling. He'd wake up crying and grappling with a fear he couldn't yet explain.

His parents, Bruce and Andrea, were worried and tried everything they could think of to comfort him, but the nightmares persisted. It wasn't until James started talking that things took a strange turn. Words like "plane" and "crash" entered his vocabulary, seemingly out of nowhere. He'd point at pictures of airplanes, almost like he knew them.

One day, he started pointing at a specific plane in a picture book and would not stop declaring, "Mine." Intrigued, his parents took him to the library and found a book full of images of World War II fighter planes. It was then that a flood of memories seemed to unlock within James. He started talking about a place called Iwo Jima, a dangerous island nicknamed "The Suck," and he spoke of taking off from a giant ship.

Things only got more interesting from there. James would now talk about the enemy plane, the explosion, and the fire. Through all of this, he was still just a toddler, but he recounted the details of a fighter pilot's death. His parents, who knew nothing about World War II or airplanes, were hooked by his specific descriptions of the type of plane, the name of the carrier, and even details about the battle.

Bruce and Andrea then began researching, trying to figure out what was happening. They discovered that the details James described matched the life and death of a real World War II pilot, James Huston Jr. The island, the plane, the carrier—it all lined up. News of the case spread, and James became a focal point for discussions on reincarnation and past life memories.

For James, it wasn't just a story. These were fragments of a life before, a life cut short. The nightmares continued but were now tinged with a strange sense of familiarity. The experience left a lasting mark—a connection to a past he was unaware of living yet somehow remembered.

What can we make of this story? Well, firstly, let's think about the concept of a unified memory that we all share. If the information and the essence of the pilot had been lost and gone with his death, then James would not have had these memories at all. For starters, we can at least understand that we are not just our physical bodies, and our existence is not limited to the lives we are living in this physical world.

Most of us consider birth as the time we were born. For me, April 18, 1957, 4:34 p.m. is right there on my birth certificate, so it must be correct, right? This must be the time of my incarnation. This is the time that was agreed on these official documents. But maybe these documents overlook a fundamental truth about who we are, where we come from, why we incarnate, and how we manifest here. Maybe, just like James, our lives have a deeper past than the official documents recognize and accept.

One question that we all ask ourselves at some point is "Who am I?" This is a very important question on our path of evolution. In our time and in our way, we have all come face to face with the essential contemplation of our being. What is the meaning of life, is there even one, and do we have a part to play in the world? Well, yes, there is meaning to life, and above that, there is meaning to your life.

Over the past 125 years, the field of psychology, and before that, philosophy and the mystical traditions, all theorized about time of birth, our evolutionary process as a species, and the vastness of the cosmos. These disciplines have looked at what we were before we became manifest on Earth and what our mission here is. The process of incarnation is important for finding our purpose in life and finding our way back to the source of everything—the black velvet void.

Trying to find your place in the world without finding where you are from can often be futile. But this chapter will discuss everything you need to know about how you moved from being light and energy, traveling from the inception of time into eternity along with the unified consciousness, to you manifesting on Earth at this time, bearing all the blessings, creativity, and brilliance that you bring with you.

There is a kaleidoscope of theories, ideas, and methodologies that have guided us along the way. Each of the great spiritual traditions speaks of an infinite universe that interconnects us all in a web of life reaching beyond our imagination, opens us to explore and question, and challenges us to evolve. Most of the ideas presented here are not new. However, for me, these thoughts, theories, and ideas are always changing, with new information challenging me to grow, let go of aspects of my experiences and education, and engage in contemplation and active inquiry with the imagination of a curious child.

I want you to also understand that we are light being manifested as physical beings. In this chapter, we extensively explore how you incarnated from being pure light to merging with the egg and sperm from your parents to create the majestic person you are today.

Everything Is Energy

The long-standing divide between science and spirituality is gradually becoming blurred, reshaping our perceptions of the universe and our identities. Spiritual wisdom that has been a part of civilization for ages is finding validation through the lens of modern quantum physics, illuminating new perspectives on reality and the essence of our existence.

Conventional physics believes that the universe is comprised of two distinct realms: matter and energy. However, quantum physics has been challenging this belief in a way that also affects our understanding of who we are. Quantum physics is perhaps the most verified of the scientific fields, and it suggests that what we perceive as matter is an illusion. When scientists had developed the methodology and equipment to understand the cells that make up everything, they launched their experiments expecting the smallest representation of matter. However, the big bodies of matter did not play along with the rules but rather bent them, and so did the quantum-sized cells. But there was a difference between the two: The elements at the center of a cell can only be measured in terms of energy charges, not through all the measurements we have for matter. In other words, at the center of every cell are energy vortexes.

I know this raises questions. You can see, touch, and feel matter, so it must be real—right? Yes, the experience we have here on Earth is valid in its physical properties. However, the reality of our world is based on energy, just like the reality of who you are is based on energy as well. The universe as you know it is made up of energy—small packs of energy vortexes that create bonds so strong and observable that they are palpable.

Science has already taught us that energy is neither created nor destroyed (Moskowitz, 2014). The same energy that existed at the beginning of time exists now, and the same process by which our universe expands outward at the speed of light also happened at our inception—or should I say at our incarnation?

In this chapter, we will explore how your light became a living organism with an energy field around it. You are energy translated into human form by the DNA of your parents, giving you a chance to learn and grow through your experience here on Earth. Let's explore these ideas and their implications for our lives.

Chakras System: Information Transmission

In the East, the guide to understanding the energy field described above is what we now call the chakra system. I know so many people talk about chakras these days, almost as if they've discovered a far-fetched and mystical concept that works in whatever way we believe. However, this is simply wrong—the chakra system is a very elaborate and intentional guide to understanding how energy flows around and within our bodies.

There are so many misconceptions about how chakras work and what they are, so let's clear those before we move along. The first of these is the most dangerous: the belief that chakras are metaphysical and have no scientific basis. Chakras have a profound effect on health and there are many documented accounts of healers diagnosing problems stemming from chakras that were later confirmed by doctors. This model is echoed in the work of others, like Carolyn Myss, who had a very famous medical intuitive program and worked closely with Dr Norm Shealy.

The intersection between the medical field and energy work has allowed us to better understand anatomy from a holistic perspective. For instance, consider how your body has nerve plexuses—networks of intersecting nerves—and endocrine glands that secrete hormones directly into the bloodstream (Groen et al., 1990). These centers of physiological activity can be linked to the different chakras in the body, creating a mirror of what is happening with the chakras within the body. Later on in the chapter, we will consider the combination of chakras, nerve plexuses, and endocrine glands and how their locations and functions seem coordinated.

When you understand both the physiological body and the human energy consciousness system (HECS), you will start to understand that it looks like the body was designed to be multidimensional and interact between the light at the core, the dimension of intention, and the human biofield. Brennan (2011b) theorized about four dimensions of humankind in her book *Light Emerging*, which explores how dimensions interact and how the foundation of the human body is constructed holographically by different frequencies of energy.

Another misconception is that chakras are only a part of New Age spirituality. While chakras have increased in popularity over the past couple of decades as they have been adopted by the Western world through the beliefs of New Age spiritualism, their significance far exceeds this. Chakras have existed since the writings of the Vedas, ancient Hindu philosophical texts that were written between 1500 and 500 B.C.E (*Sanskrit*, n.d.).

So, now that we have looked at what the chakra system is not, let's talk about what it is. Derived from the Sanskrit word for "wheel" or "disc," the chakras are vital energy centers that reside along the subtle body—the energy body. There are seven chakras, each associated with specific physical, emotional, and spiritual attributes. These energy centers act as conduits for the flow of vital life force energy throughout the body.

I know most pictures you have seen probably show chakras as glowing wheels distributed from the base of the spine to the top of the head, but chakras do not look exactly like that. Instead, think about how a picture of the circulatory system on paper would be in 2D, but how within your body the veins go everywhere, in 3D. In the same way, your chakras have depth—they are not just balls of energy in a straight line. They go through your body holographically like vortexes and lead to a metaphysical system that emanates through your body. The body manifests itself from the energy field and storehouse of information in the DNA. The human biofield is the messenger for the DNA and transmits the resonant frequencies of all the organs and systems.

As stated previously, this process starts at the cellular division stage, where the centripetal and centrifugal forces activate the information codes in the DNA so they can start taking effect and manifesting in your body. The energy directs the process of cell division and makes it possible for the information to come alive within the dividing cells.

The upper chakras—the upper part of the double torus—represent the divine order to the lower chakras—"as above, so below." The root and the crown chakras each have one opening, with the root chakra's opening being like a vortex facing down but funneling into an energy nerve that runs up the body to expand into the outward-facing crown chakra. These two chakras are very important as they help with the transference or incarnation of your soul into this world. When you are born, the crown chakra is wider so your guides can safely escort you to this world. As you grow, the root chakra starts to develop until you are grounded, or rooted to this physical world.

Between the root and the crown chakras are five others that also help you move successfully from the astral plane into this one. These look like vortexes with two ends, one to your front and the other to your back. They all merge at the center, where the energy nerve runs from the root to the crown. Each chakra corresponds to unique qualities and aspects of your being, including physical health, emotional stability, mental clarity, and spiritual growth. We will go over these functions in more detail as we explore how you move from the astral plane into this one through incarnation.

The chakras are connected to your energy field in the same way that your body parts are a part of your physical body. You eat, breathe, exercise, and balance out your physical health through the actions of your body, and your energy field can also be balanced, changed, and improved through the actions of your chakras. At any time, these chakras can be either overactive or underactive, leading to imbalances in the energy flow. Emotional traumas, negative thought patterns, and environmental factors can contribute to blockages within your chakras, impeding the natural flow of energy from the collective consciousness and the infinite universe.

The interconnected nature of the chakra system emphasizes a holistic approach to healing. Since the chakras are connected not only to your biological body but also to your emotional, etheric, mental, astral, and celestial bodies, healing channeled through the chakra system will affect your whole being. Think of it this way: If your car keeps breaking down because its fuel system is not efficient, then only looking at the cooling system or the electric connections will not solve the problem. The underlying issue might manifest in some blown fuses or overheating within the electric and cooling systems, but resolving these will not fix the actual problem.

The same thing happens when you rely only on your physical body to understand yourself. Your physical body will reflect what is happening in your other bodies, but that does not mean the problem can be solved at the physical level. Through the chakra system, as it pertains to the energy field around you, you can bring holistic alignment to your whole being that will impact your physical body.

The chakra system is crucial to everything I have learned and taught about energy healing. It's a different way of looking at the body's anatomy that is not just one-dimensional. I hope more people will discover that the synergy between chakra healing and energy medicine offers a transformative pathway to inner healing and self-discovery.

The chakra system is also very important in your incarnation, as it is the gateway through which you enter this world. The forces created by the vortexes merge the DNA print from your parents with your divine essence, allowing the cells to divide and create your physical body. We will cover this concept in the next chapter, but for now, let's look at the other two higher dimensions of the HECS.

In the previous chapter, when we looked at the chakras we discussed how they are two-way doors, bringing information through from the infinite universe and recording information from your interactions onto the A-field. This dual opposing functionality of the chakras is important for allowing your core to holographically appear in human form, where the higher realms of the divine mind, divine love, and the divine plan can inform the lower realms. The fulcrum of interaction happens at the fourth level or the astral plane, where your light, and your intention to incarnate as a blessing unto your family and this world, enters the Earth plane.

Remember, you are like an avatar, and the divine mind is your source and your permanent home. You are only visiting this world, bringing with you special gifts, talents, and ideas that will impact humanity and help advance us to the next stage in the evolution of humanity. To journey to this world, though, there is quite a bit that happens. In *Hands of Light* (Brennan, 2011a) talks about meeting your spirit guides at the beginning of your journey.

The Case of Musaigwa

Musaigwa is a native traditional healer from Seke, a small, remote village in Southern Africa. According to Musaigwa, he had been pursuing a career in farming for a very long time, but he'd hardly seen any success. When he got to his mid-30s, he got very sick and was bedridden for a while. He had no idea what was wrong with him, but he had an intuition that if he understood his roots, he would find a way to connect with his body and channel the healing he wanted.

He then started on a path to find out who he was through meditation. Musaigwa was and still is illiterate, so he did not have any books to explain these ideas to him. His entire experience was spiritual, just as is the case in many other stories like his from all over the world. I love his story because it has an authenticity to it that is hard to find these days. His experience was uninformed—or inspired.

Anyway, after a couple of months, he started to have dreams in which he would meet with his guides and they would tell him what to do. To begin with, they showed him a plant that could heal him. Initially, he was skeptical, just as you and I would be as well. Eventually, out of desperation, he went out and found the tree and prepared it as he had been told in the dream. After taking the potion, he started to miraculously recover, and within a few weeks he was healthy again.

This is not where the story ends, though. Even after he had been healed, his guides continued to show up in his dreams and started to show him more and more plants that could be used for healing different ailments. After some time, all the people in his village would go to Musaigwa for healing, and a while after that, people began to travel to see him from all over. He is now a healer working to help people get their health back, after understanding the assignment from his guides.

I know Musaigwa might not even know this yet, but the work he is doing now has always been his path. It was not chosen for him randomly, but rather he agreed to and chose that path before he left for this world. It is the same for all of us—we have a specific task that we agreed to do and that we came to do here on Earth. Yes, you also have a guide, and if you ask them to, they can help you to review your path and how you walk on it. I recall Brennan (2011a) saying:

> Then I began seeing spiritual beings, as if in a vision. Then I began to hear them talking to me and feel them touch me. I now accept that I have a guide. I can see, hear, and feel him. "He" says he is not male or female. "He" says that in his world there is no splitting along sexual lines and that beings at his level of existence are whole. "He" says that his name is Heyoan, which means, "The Wind Whispering Truth Through the Centuries." His introduction to me was slow and organic. The nature of our relationship grows daily, as I am guided to new levels of understanding. (p. 14)

These guides are there to remind most of us of who we are and what our purpose is. Sometimes, they will manifest in our lives, as they did for Musaigwa and Barbara Brennan. However, most of the time these guides communicate through your hara to bring the inspiration into your heart, rather than directly to your physical dimension.

This is a very common experience. Have you ever felt deeply like you were being called to do something? That tugging is your guide or guides communicating to you. How you see and understand this will differ depending on your background, but in Christianity, the common term is "spirit." The spirit of God calls you to follow the path that you are supposed to follow, and it guides you as you do so.

I relate to this so much at my current stage in life. Just a few months before I started writing this book, I had decided to retire. I was so happy with the work I had done and excited to see how others would carry it on and continue to increase the collective awareness of humanity. I will forever be grateful for all the experiences I have had and the lives I have impacted. It's such a humbling feeling to know I have been able to impact someone.

Just as I was about to pull out my itinerary for retirement, though, the spirit called me to come back to my work again. If I'd had to make the call purely based on my human logical thinking, I would not have done so. However, my spirit called me to get back and share the truths that I had learned, building on the work of others who had gone before me. This is why I have written this book, and will be working on others that are on the way. I have a mission that I know I have to finish.

We are all called in different ways. While some follow their guides physically, others follow them in dreams, and others follow the instruction and desire emanating from their core star, we are all the same. I want you to think about the following question very carefully: What should you be doing that your spirit keeps telling you to do?

That is a powerful start. Most of the time, we do not even take time to rest and listen to our spirits or ask this type of question. I dare you to sit in silence for about five minutes and see if your higher dimensions will trickle the answer down to your physical mind. It's okay—you can do this right now. Slide in your bookmark and zone out for a moment.

So, you have a mission that you agreed to at the beginning of time and that you came to Earth to fulfill. That is amazing. While your soul has already moved from the astral plane and incarnated here, you can still access and receive information from the divine mind, from your guide. To understand how, let's look at how the chakras move information through the body, starting with the idea of centripetal and centrifugal forces in the chakras.

Centripetal & Centrifugal Forces in Chakras

This is one of Walter Russell's ideas that I have been contemplating quite a bit lately. Through my experience working with the human energy consciousness system, I keep seeing more and more functionality in the idea that each chakra point has two ends that converge at the center. This creates two forces within the vortex: one pulling toward your physical dimension and the other pulling away from it. This is where the chakra seals between the dimensions reside.

This double action is crucial for the movement of information through the chakra system. To best understand it, I want you to think of two opposite forces in physics: centripetal and centrifugal. Centripetal force makes things go in a circle. When a mass moves in a circle, like when you drive a car around a bend, the force that pulls it toward the center of the circle is called centripetal force. It's like the car is being tugged toward the middle of the curve so it doesn't fly off the road. On the other hand, centrifugal force is inertia. Imagine spinning a bucket of water around; the water will try to move outwards, away from the center. This feeling of things moving away from the center is what we call centrifugal force.

These forces are essential in understanding the dynamics of rotating or revolving objects, one example of which is a vortex. Just as centripetal force pulls objects toward the center of their circular path, the practice of focusing on chakras through meditation and yoga can be seen as a way of drawing energy inward, toward yourself. Remember the A-field or the collective subconscious in psychology—these are the repositories for energy that we pull from. This inward focus helps integrate and harmonize various aspects of our being, allowing us to pull into our reality the frequency of the A-field that we want to see manifest.

Let's journey back to the idea of the the Big Bang and the Big Breath. When life exploded onto the scene, there was an equal and opposite reaction that created dark matter equal to the matter that exists in this world. Think of it this way—the same explosion that we picture as being light had an opposite that created dark matter. It took the two opposing forces to create life, and the same is true when you are created in your mother's womb.

Here is my theory, and I invite you to research it further: When the light meets with the DNA during conception, there is an explosion just like at the beginning of time, and it is these opposing forces that combust to create life. From then onward, the combustion remains present within the vortexes that are part of your chakra system. We cannot overstate the importance of seeing the chakra points as vortexes rather than just as discs that are distributed along our bodies. As an energy healer, when you hover your hand over a chakra point, you can feel the pull of the vortex and you can transmit light into it.

Next, we will look at all the chakras individually, discussing how they function and correlate to your physical body, and their role in the human biofield.

Root Chakra: Muladhara

The root chakra is also known as Muladhara, and its hue is a bright crimson red. This chakra connects to your adrenal glands in the body, right at the base of your spine, giving you a sense of stability and security. When you think about this chakra, think about your survival instinct. It's like the foundation of a house, keeping you grounded and stable. Our bodies need to be earthed so we can properly bring our light into this natural experience.

Sacral Chakra: Svadhisthana

The sacral chakra, or Svadhisthana, is the orange energy vortex. This chakra is linked to the gonads. It resides in the lower abdomen area and is tied to your emotions and creativity. It's like a well of emotions that can affect your relationships and the pleasure you find in life. When this chakra is balanced, you may feel more inspired and connected to your creative side.

Solar Plexus Chakra: Manipura

Moving up, we come to the solar plexus chakra, known as Manipura. This chakra radiates a sunny yellow color. It's associated with the pancreas. Found in the upper abdomen area, this chakra is all about personal power. When this chakra is in harmony, you may feel a boost in self-confidence and willpower. It's like having a strong core that empowers your actions and decisions.

Heart Chakra: Anahata

The heart chakra, also called Anahata, is represented by the color green. This chakra's connection is with the thymus gland. Located at the center of the chest, it resonates with love and compassion. When your heart chakra is balanced, you may feel a deep sense of connection and harmony with yourself and others. It's all about fostering love and understanding in all aspects of life.

Throat Chakra: Vishuddha

Moving to the throat chakra, known as Vishuddha, we encounter a soothing blue color. This chakra links to the thyroid gland and is positioned in the throat area. It's all about communication, helping you express yourself authentically. When this chakra is balanced, you may find it easier to speak your truth and communicate effectively with those around you.

Third-Eye Chakra: Ajna

Next, we find the third-eye chakra, or Ajna, which shines with an indigo hue. This chakra is connected to the pituitary gland and is situated between the eyes on the forehead. It's linked to intuition and insight, providing a gateway to your inner wisdom and imagination. When in balance, this chakra can enhance your clarity of thought and deep intuition.

Crown Chakra: Sahasrara

Finally, at the top, we have the crown chakra, known as Sahasrara. This chakra is represented by the colors violet and white, and is associated with the pineal gland. Located at the crown of the head, it's all about spirituality and connection to the Divine and to universal energy. When this chakra is aligned, you may feel a profound sense of oneness with the world around you, tapping into the vast energy of the universe.

The truth of our origins and fate can completely change our lives; it has changed countless lives already. The idea that we are merely mechanical biological creatures with no soul or meaning outside of what we know in this lifetime is just wrong. The science of our bodies and how they relate to our consciousness adamantly supports that we are more than the shells we are in right now.

You are the light that needs to shine. You are connected to higher levels of consciousness, which you can access. All of this is available to you as a birthright. As your parents conceived you, the divine mind imprinted your light onto the DNA of the sperm and egg, and the miracle that brought the expanse of the universe to life became alive in you—that is divine wisdom.

PART 3

Chapter 6:

Family Systems: Awakening the Divine Genogram

In the introduction to this book, and in my first book, *Blessings From a Thousand Generations*, I talk about how family systems helped me find my past so I could start moving toward my future. The journey to discovering our cosmic greatness starts with exploring and understanding who we are, part of which is grounded in who we have been in the past. Not just that, but also how our ancestors shaped the heritage into which we were born.

While we are individuals, we are nested in the bonds that were created by our parents, uncles, aunts, and the rest of our family. Beyond that, we are also influenced by the environment we grew up in, without even noticing it. Unfortunately, sometimes the family love bonds that intertwine with our heritage are not in line with the divine will that the infinite universe has for us. Because of this, we can end up cut off from the light that should be guiding us from within. We end up cut off from our divine genogram.

The way heritage works is a lot like the five monkeys experiment discussed by Maestripieri (2012). In this famous experiment—

which was originally run by Gordon Stephenson in the 1960s, before public sentiment turned the scientific community away from experimenting on animals in this way—five monkeys were taken and locked up in a cage. In the middle of the cage was a ladder, and at the top of the ladder was a nice fresh banana that would get switched out for a fresher one now and then. As soon as the monkeys saw the banana, they rushed to climb the ladder and grab it, but they were immediately hosed down with ice-cold water. This kept happening until most of the monkeys stopped trying to get the banana altogether, but this was not so for some of them. Now and then, there would be one monkey that would still try to go up the ladder, which would mean all of the monkeys would get hosed down.

It got to the point where if one of the monkeys even walked too close to the ladder, all the other monkeys would help to pull back that monkey and beat it up. Since they now understood that they would all be hosed down with cold water if one of them tried to get the banana, they figured out that if they prevented any monkey from climbing the ladder, they would all be safe. After this, none of the monkeys would even dare try to go up the ladder despite there being a nice banana at the top.

Now, here is where things got interesting. One day, the experimenters removed one of the monkeys and replaced it with a new monkey that didn't know the ice-cold water rule. As soon as it got into the cage, the new monkey went for the banana, but the others pulled it down and beat it up. It tried again a few times, but it would always get pulled down and beaten up. So, this monkey now understood that it should not try to go up the ladder.

The new monkey never experienced the ice-cold showers, but it learned not to go up the ladder regardless. And things only got more interesting from there. The researchers removed another of the original monkeys and replaced it with a second new one. The results were the same: The new monkey tried to go up the ladder and get the banana, and it got beaten up as well—only this time, the first new monkey joined in the beating. The cycle was repeated until all the original monkeys had been taken out of the cage and none of the new monkeys had any experience with the cold water.

The tradition carried on, though: Whenever a monkey was added to the cage, the others would beat it away from the ladder, even though none of them had any idea why this was being done. None of them knew about the cold water, but they gave up on reaching the banana and stopped others from doing so as well. The beating of each new monkey did not seem to have any personal negative emotions attached to it, and the monkeys got along fairly well except when it came to the ladder and the banana.

So, what does this have to do with you and family systems? Well, in the same way that the new monkey was introduced to the cage, you were introduced to the world in a family that already had its set of beliefs. Those beliefs and past experiences can hinder you from reaching out toward your destiny or letting your light shine. Now, hopefully your family will not pull you down physically and beat you up every time you are about to succeed. However, their beliefs and negative bonds can affect how you perceive the world and approach life. This can then lead to a serious blockage in your human biofield, making it hard for you to display the light that is within. You can get lost in the noise of humanity and forget to live up to your divine genome—your true self.

In this chapter, we will look at family systems and consider how they may be helping or stopping us from chasing our divinity. You need to remember your divinity and break free from everything that might be holding you back from performing at your peak. Being in touch with your divine genome can help you become more creative, productive, focused, and resilient in chasing your goals. It sets you on a path of greatness and, even better than that, it helps you to pull others up the ladder with you to get their own banana as well.

Expansion & Integration of Family Systems

Family systems have their early foundations in the work of Sigmund Freud from the late 19th and early 20th centuries. His psychoanalytic theory laid the groundwork. Psychoanalytic theory is a framework that explores how human behavior is influenced by unconscious thoughts, desires, and motivations. It emphasizes the role of the unconscious mind, childhood experiences, and internal conflicts in shaping personality and behavior. Freud believed that unresolved conflicts from early childhood could lead to psychological problems later in life, and that therapy could help individuals gain insight into their unconscious processes to achieve personal growth and healing.

He was right, but he overlooked the reality that these conflicts in childhood would block the child from bringing their true potential to light. After resolving their conflicts, it was therefore also necessary to help individuals discover their cosmic potential and energy. Freud renamed the life force or prana referred to in ancient texts as the id—the unbridled energy that needed to be mediated by the ego. His focus shifted, leaving many of his theories to be explored by other analysts. For example, his theory on the libido was explored by Wilhelm Reich, who contributed to the field of mind-body psychotherapy.

In the 1950s, Gregory Bateson, an anthropologist, started to apply systems theory to human behavior. His work on communication and cybernetics provided a foundation for understanding families as systems with patterns of interactions and feedback loops, very similar to computer systems. This meant we could study these patterns in therapy and use them to help improve the psychological health of our clients. Alongside Bateson, in the late 1940s to the 1960s Murray Bowen applied the systems approach to families, creating eight identifiable components in family therapy. These ranged from sibling positions, triangle relationships, the nuclear family emotional process, and emotional cutoff, to name a few. Yet the model bypassed the spiritual potential within the family system and each individual as part of the whole; nor did Bateson, Bowen, or Minuchin address the primary spiritual foundation of the transgenerational legacy.

Tele in Family Systems

Alongside the burgeoning field of psychology, from as early as 1921 Jacob Moreno, who attended lectures with Freud, branched off and developed his "psychodrama" modality. His contribution to the field is important to note, as he introduced the idea of "tele," an invisible communication that seems to be transmitted between members. This provided a significant insight into the quantum realm, along with Carl Jung's theory on the collective unconscious.

Let's think through everything we have learned. In physics, there is a concept called quantum entanglement that shows us how, once two photons or atoms are intertwined, they remain connected through a seemingly metaphysical connection, despite the distance between them. In addition, religion refers to the existence of multiple realms that are holographically interwoven with each other, and we exist in those realms in multiple forms. Furthermore, there is the collective consciousness in psychology, and there is the A-field. When you integrate everything, you can see how the existence of a network that underpins everything we know starts to form.

Unlike with one-sided attractions or projections, tele involves a mutual invisible transmission between two family members or two people. It can be positive (attraction) or negative (repulsion), but it always involves a bidirectional flow of emotions. Moreno (1964) argues that you cannot fake these feelings: Tele arises spontaneously and authentically, reflecting the genuine and immediate emotional state of the individuals involved. In group psychodrama, participants are part of a collective field, and they interact with it based upon their previous relational positive or negative love bonds.

Tele plays a key role in forming the structure of relationships within a group—family or otherwise. Positive tele leads to cohesion and strong bonds, while negative tele can create distance and conflict. Understanding tele helps in navigating and managing these group dynamics. What is fascinating is that Moreno's discovery of tele and his life's work seem to have evolved along with Bert Hellinger's family constellations therapy. Let's explore some of the underpinnings and evolution of Hellinger's model next.

Constellations in Family Systems

Building on Freud's foundations, Alfred Adler introduced the idea of family constellations. This was the first theory to prioritize birth order and sibling relationships in personality development. Alfred viewed the family as a system where each member had an influence on the next, depending on their role in the family and influence over the other. Under his theory, we realize that younger siblings are more likely to look up to their older siblings, not the other way around.

Adler's ideas coincided with work by Bert Hellinger, a German psychotherapist who developed family constellations (Manné, 2009) that map out the connections within a family in the same way that the stars map out information in the sky. This creates a blueprint that the psychologist can use to deal with deeply rooted family issues. Hellinger's therapeutic method seeks to reveal and address hidden dynamics within a family system, almost like laying out the connections, sensing the family's energy field dynamics, and then looking closely at the map to see where unhealthy patterns might emerge.

From my perspective, family constellations work identifies the invisible transmission of transgenerational patterns that entangle each generation. The approach outlined by Hellinger is based on the belief that family problems and dysfunctions can be transmitted energetically through generations, often unconsciously, affecting the lives of descendants decades or even centuries later. I have identified these patterns as positive and negative love bonds, which suppress the divine qualities of each family member throughout the generations and stay within the family mind field until the divine qualities are restored and reconciliation occurs. Here, the true transfiguration occurs, healing both past and future generations and contributing to the evolution of humanity.

Hellinger's claim was a profound one to make. Biology at that time was way behind and could not substantiate that a psychological problem could be transmitted from generation to generation. However, the idea that love bonds could be transmitted was taught by our great ancestors from every culture and understood by our ancient religious traditions. In Hinduism, the idea of generational curses can be seen in the story of how Gandhari cursed Lord Krishna's house and bloodline. The Bible mentions generational sin in Exodus 20:5, which states that "the iniquities of the fathers are visited upon the sons and daughters—unto the third and fourth generation" (*Holy Bible, New International Version*, 2013/1973). Now, when you read this, it might sound like God was just really out to get people for their sins in the worst way possible. But it is not like that at all.

The passage in Exodus is there not as a curse but rather as a warning. If you sin and fix your mind in the realm of one sin or another, then you invite that sin to take hold of your family and influence what happens not only to you but also to subsequent generations. This has remained true to this day: We transmit the positive and negative aspects of our lives to our children and our grandchildren, regardless of whether we know it. It's like the experiment with the monkeys we explored earlier in the chapter: You can leave subsequent generations in situations that they do not understand, but they will still act according to invisible transgenerational patterns.

This idea has been very powerful for thousands of years, before the theories of quantum entanglement and family constellations. From here on, however, many studies were conducted proving that psychological conditions could indeed be traced in families through the generations. Take, for example, a study by Yehuda and Lehrner (2018) that looked at intergenerational transmission of trauma effects and the possible role of epigenetic mechanisms in this transmission. The evidence for the transmission of family patterns through generations is a fact. The question then is, what is the medium for the movement of the information? The goal of family constellations is to uncover the dynamics and bring resolution and healing while answering this question as well. Think about how you can cry watching a sad movie or feel happy watching a comedy. You know the emotions are coming from a fake depiction of reality, but still, you have an emotional response. Like quantum entanglement, the actors' emotional expressions are transmitted through the A-field, matching a similar resonance within us.

In a family, however, these connections are much stronger and the effect is therefore much more noticeable. It's like the difference between how the Moon acts around the Earth and how an asteroid much further away would behave. The closer a node is in the system, the more it is affected by the action of the other node. Because of this, the negative effects not only move from one person to the next, but they compound and move from one generation to the next. Dysfunctional patterns can be carried over from previous generations, influencing present relationships and behaviors.

These transgenerational traumas often then manifest as personal or relational issues in the new generation. The method of rediscovering our divine genogram acknowledges the influence of our ancestors and the importance of understanding their roles and experiences to resolve current issues. The idea that our ancestors are looking over us is common across most cultures. It's believed that there is a cloud where all the ancestors go, and from there they communicate with us and bring us wisdom.

There is a truth to this. While our ancestors move on from this life and reunite their spirit with the infinite universe, the combined energy of their constellations leaves an imprint in the A-field. It is this imprint or program you incarnate into, so you are always influenced and informed by the heritage your ancestors imprinted within your DNA, your family mind field, and the collective A-Field. I imagine there are fields among fields, interwoven into a tapestry of the holographic universe.

Now, imagine if you could reclaim the divinity residing within the quantum entanglements, freeing your divine qualities and transfiguring your negative love bonds. This is the evolution that humanity is ready to embrace in order to reclaim and fully incarnate the radiance emerging from within. It is here that the divine genogram moves us toward a unified healing approach, where we can dive deeper into our divine heritage and our cosmic origins and allow ourselves to radiate divinity, cohesiveness, and coherence. Let's explore the family biofield and divine genogram and why restoring the divine qualities is essential to the evolution and enlightenment of humanity.

In family constellation sessions, just like in psychodrama, those present act as representatives for your family members or elements of your issue. This process allows you to observe and understand your family blueprint as you watch the interaction. Hellinger put forward that a "knowing field" emerges during constellations, where representatives can intuitively access information about the family dynamics they are representing, often revealing unconscious patterns. The "knowing field" is a recreation of the A-field, and the participants' human biofields interact with a specific part of the A-field.

Think of it this way: When you consciously and unconsciously interact with the A-field, you are able to know things about others that you have no other way of knowing. This knowledge does not always come to you traditionally, via the five senses, but it may arise in you as intuition. What was happening in the sessions Hellinger describes, I propose, is that the participant's biofield was "tele" communicating invisible signals, blending and matching with others within the collective group consciousness. The meta-communication between and among systems was transmitting memory signals, and people would step unknowingly into a constellation that awakened a part of their own narrative. When they were in the session, members often said things they would have otherwise never known, and they even changed their tone and voices at times. The constellation process has brought to light hidden family dynamics and facilitated healing movements for so many people.

Therapeutic Process in Family Constellations

Therapy sessions for family constellations are very interesting. The client, who is referred to as the seeker, describes their situation to the group. The facilitator guides the client to allocate key family members or elements related to the issue to the participants, who are positioned in the space according to the seeker's perception or the facilitator's intuition. As the representatives take their places, they begin to experience feelings and reactions that reflect the family dynamics.

Both the seeker and the facilitator then observe the interactions and movements of the representatives. The facilitator may ask the representatives to express their feelings or make specific statements to reveal deeper dynamics, and will also guide the process to acknowledge and honor past traumas, resolve entanglements, and restore balance to the client's life. This may involve physical movements, spoken acknowledgments, or symbolic acts to represent reconciliation and healing.

Hellinger's family constellations not only provided a profound and innovative approach to understanding and resolving family dynamics, but in the process also opened a doorway to even deeper ideas. As we accept the nature of family systems, we also understand the broader nature of the A-field and the human biofield. Hellinger's work offers a path to healing that honors and respects the interconnectedness of all family members, past and present. This approach has enriched the field of family systems therapy, providing valuable insights and tools for therapists and clients alike. What would happen if we added one more step to this—after making amends with the past, can we then start to unravel the divinity that is hidden within?

By now, family systems had introduced several theories that changed people's lives. Before family systems, there wasn't a model for people to explore what had happened in their past or how transgenerational patterns were influencing their physical, emotional, psychological, relational, social, and spiritual well-being. Evolution within the field, and also in neurobiology and physics, has invited us to explore new paradigm shifts, such as the A-field—as previously mentioned. In addition to being a memory field network of all information that has ever existed, the A-field also has subgroupings that function as smaller A-fields for families, social networks, and communities.

Over a century, the burgeoning field of psychology has moved through several forces, from behaviorism (monkey experiment) to psychoanalytic (Freudian), humanistic (Rogerian and family systems), and transpersonal. Family systems theories, like family constellations and internal family systems, offer both a humanistic and a person-centered approach. As we move forward, I will introduce the divine genogram as an additional transpersonal model, where we reclaim our innate divine qualities and our spiritual birthright.

One of the things I am interested in is seeing leaders in our communities, societies, and countries, as well as in the corporate world, help people reach their potential by considering the influence of family systems and the collective divine genogram (the divine potential hidden within any conflict).

Family Biofield: The Divine Genogram

So, what is a family biofield? Well, remember how we are all made of energy and have a human biofield emanating from us? That field interacts with the fields of the people we are close to, creating a system that functions as a unit. Consider for a moment how, when trauma happens to one person in a family, it is transmitted through the system and impacts everyone. The family's collective mind field adapts to both the conscious and unconscious transmission of a traumatic event. Beyond consciousness, family members are impacted by generational trauma and family secrets, which become shared stored memories that impact behavior. These traumas are held within the collective mind field or the A-field, which holographically connects all sentient life.

Have you ever felt like something was wrong with a sibling or someone you are close to, and then you found out they were not feeling well? This is a very common phenomenon, especially with very close relatives. The reason for this is that there is a lot of entanglement between the two human biofields; from what we've learned from the quantum entanglement theory, it follows that, regardless of distance, the two beings are always connected.

Beyond traditional psychological and system methodologies that provide insight, understanding, and healing, there are mystical and spiritual reasons why certain souls come together as a family. Remember that every family member came as a blessing, to bring light and healing and help untangle the hidden divinity and potential within the family. The view that the family is a complex, emotional, psychological, relational, and spiritual unit of consciousness provides the narrative that will unlock your divine potential.

This connection is like an invisible web that connects families and other groups of people who are close—it is not only about biological connections. Let's reflect on a few stories. In my family of origin, the circumstances around my birth and my father's adoption history were hidden threads of family secrets. In my husband's family, there was a secret about an affair my father-in-law had after my husband's birth. The story is long, and most of the details are available elsewhere. Anyway, my husband's first marriage was to a Las Vegas dancer, with whom he eloped and had a wonderful son, Matthew David. My husband's decisions cost him a respected position within the family business. It wasn't until a few years after his father's death that we were contacted and informed that my father-in-law had also had a secret: He'd had an affair with a dancer, who had a son. At the time, my father-in-law was told that if he left his wife to marry the dancer, he would be disowned from the family business. As you can see, this family secret was re-enacted by my husband. These types of hidden secrets are pervasive throughout humanity. Understanding the narrative is one aspect; uncovering the divine qualities of trust, love and acceptance, respect, and relational love are other aspects, and can take some time to achieve. Regardless of the situations we were born into, we came as a blessing of love and light.

In the evolution of my work, I discovered that family systems models can be both transformational and transcendent. Yet for deeper transfiguration, we need to access the hidden fields that entangle us in negative love bonds, hindering the fullness of our incarnation and the transmission of all the frequencies inherent in the divine qualities. The emergence of these qualities is our birthright. We came as a blessing, and there are thousands of blessings coming to us. All the prayers from all the generations, and all the cultures too, are here for us to tap into. Our heritage is rich in blessings that awaken us from profound forgetting.

We need to unearth the negative love bonds and explore our transgenerational past to unveil our divine nature. From a transformative perspective, these models identify secrets, trauma, and unhealthy coping methods, as well as providing relief and change. From years of working with thousands of students and clients at the level of the human energy consciousness system (HECS), it became apparent that a transpersonal perspective was needed to reclaim our innate divine birthright by releasing the divine qualities within the family. Most therapists address patterns that can be identified in many families; they provide insight and relief, even changing people's lives and behavior, yet they may miss the restoration process of light. Restoring the light within the individual, family, and collective fields moves us toward transmuting centuries of trauma to reclaim our innate divine nature.

Moreover, exploring and healing the negative love bonds can free you from the transgenerational patterns of blame, hate, resentment, rage, and destructive behaviors that suppress the divine qualities within you, your family, and your ancestors. Entangled within the family field are the innate divine qualities, awaiting reconciliation and restoration. Take some time to research and explore how your past might have influenced your present situation. From here, you can uncover the light that wants to radiate through you. When this light radiates, it brings with it purpose, and it holographically raises the vibrational frequency of every member of your family.

Family Systems & the Seven Stages of Incarnation

Let's look at family systems within the context of the HECS and the seven stages of incarnation. From the physical perspective, our family genogram offers us insight into our earthly family existence, providing the background and historical foundation of our family. The HECF provides us with insight into the family field, which transmits our emotional, psychological, relational, and spiritual health. In the haric dimension, we can identify both the positive and negative intentions expressed within the family's collective field. Finally, at the core star level, each member's core star either radiates or is shrouded by transgenerational family and social trauma.

The infinite intelligent field, which provides transfigurative love and the divine design of humanity, resides deeper than the genetic codes recorded within our DNA. The fabric of the universe is teeming with life energy—divine energy that is your birthright. DNA provides the divine framework and historical record of our human existence, while beneath the code is the Flower of Life transmitting our cosmic divine origins. Now is the time to unify physics and spirituality to understand humanity's true origins.

Have you ever wondered why many religious traditions refer to God, Brahma, Krishna, Mohammed, and Earth as our spiritual parents, and why we say things like "Mother Earth" and "Father God"? While the infinite universe and the Heavenly Father are not male, and the Earth is not female, we use these terms nonetheless. As children growing up, our parents are like the masculine and feminine face of God. As adults, we unconsciously use masculine and feminine to describe spiritual phenomena. In ancient Chinese philosophy, these two opposing forces are referred to as "yin and yang." Interestingly enough, quantum physics has shown two entangled photons that appear as the yin and yang symbol (Turner, 2023). In short, we believe that since we have a father and a mother here on Earth, then the cosmic energy that brought us forth must be one of these two genders.

It is not so. There is no gender to the fabric of energy that you come from. It simply is what God said to Moses when he asked for his name: "I AM, that which I AM" (*Holy Bible, New International Version*, 2013/1973, Exodus 3:7). The word for God in the earliest Torah manuscripts, Elohim, is neither male nor female, but plural (Shvat, 2016). We all come from another parentage, other than the one you know about. You are from light, and you are light. This is the part of you that needs to come to the light. Despite what your family systems look like or what you have been through, you cannot neglect this simple truth nor stop the pursuit of it. Each of us is part of a unified intelligent field teeming with omnipotent light, love, wisdom, and grace.

The Divine Genogram

My divine genogram theory emerged from an integration of family systems with HECS, ancient wisdom traditions, and biblical principles. It was evident that transformation and some healing were taking place within each of these methodologies—yet, for me, an essential element was missing.

Within the family field, it was clear that certain divine qualities were shrouded. The light within the family was entangled in negative love bonds that held the mystery of light and the full incarnation process. For the alchemical process of transfiguration to take place, however, something beyond transformation and transcendence was needed. Exploring these narratives with traditional psychological modalities, family systems models, and transpersonal models guided us to where we are today, and these models are a part of our heritage and the evolution of humanity. However, exploring our cosmic and divine origins now requires a paradigm shift. Is it possible to fully radiate all the light we came to bless our family and earth? Remember, we came as blessings, to bring light, hope, and healing to our family and the world. Navigating becoming human wasn't the easiest journey for some of us, and it was even harder for others. What if there was a simpler way to unravel the mystery, to remember and awaken the light within you? I would guess you would want to explore this idea and practice some simple self-healing meditations that awaken the light within while balancing the polarity that keeps you separate from your core.

The re-emergence of the divine qualities and the family field of light is needed for generational change and is also necessary for the evolution of humanity. Returning to the greater mystery of light that may have been shrouded for generations can be freeing for the individual, their relatives, their descendants, and their ancestors. It was through the application of these principles in my life, in my private practice, and in teaching students that the divine genogram offered another level of transfiguration and healing.

In *Blessings From a Thousand Generations*, I map out my family genogram and the evolution of the God-realization genogram. In the second edition, I rename the process as the divine genogram or genome. The focus is on exploring both the transformation and transcendence process as a guide and practice that eventually leads you toward the transfiguration process—uncovering the light within and radiating all of your divine qualities.

In my personal God-realization genogram, I transfigured the shroud of hidden secrets, painful abandonments, adoptions, and rejections. The process led to me untangling aspects of transfigurative love that were hidden beneath unearthed pain, shame, and sorrow. My contribution to family systems is to propose the divine genogram as an update to the previous model—to identify and restore the inherent divine qualities waiting to be unearthed, like fine gems beneath the rich soil of life lessons. When they are restored through the chakra system and into the family field, a rebirth happens: The light of who you are and who you have always been radiates through. The struggles and hardships of your family become a guidepost leading you toward the reclamation process. You no longer cling to outdated labels like "dysfunctional" but find a new way to understand how love is bonded within your family. Your divine birthright emerges from the core of your being.

If you are reading these words, you are already contemplating this process in your own family. You may already recognize some of the positive and negative generational patterns as you read. Remember, as you start this process, to give yourself time and space—and perhaps ask for support if what arises seems overwhelming or too painful to do alone.

I encourage you to take each step at your own pace, knowing that you are worth it. Taking your first steps offers you an opportunity to explore new concepts, like understanding your generational family field, which is always challenging. In addition, you can begin to see and explore the astral collective field, spheres of consciousness, and the A-field. You may begin to awaken a new awareness of more influences on how we think and feel about ourselves and others, as we discussed in a previous chapter. It is important to acknowledge that these collective bands of consciousness have an impact on us.

Consider the massive difference in how two people can understand or interpret an interaction based on the love bonds in their family. Let's say that in a meeting, the boss points out that the last annual performance was poor and that the company might need to find ways to recover from the bad year. If you are in the meeting and you come from a family that had a negative love bond of lack of trust and support, you may think the remarks are aimed at you. You may start to think the boss is against you and wants to get rid of you because you are not enough. Because of the negative love bonds you were born into, you believe your boss thinks you are the problem. You conjure up a false narrative hidden within your past experience.

In contrast, if there are positive love bonds of support and trust in your family, you could see the entire ordeal differently. You might think that the only reason your boss even said this was so you could help come up with solutions to the problem. You will see your boss in the same way your parents saw you, as encouraging and supportive.

You can always reflect on how the negative and positive love bonds manifest in your life. Are there already patterns that you can identify within your family—an addiction maybe, a psychological behavior, or a pattern of actions? Oftentimes, before you even start to map out the blueprint of your family system, you will be able to tell what these love bonds are. Consider keeping a journal as you walk through this observation and inquiry process.

What does all this mean for you and your divine genogram? Perhaps you are now excited to explore the invisible web within your family's mind field. Or, if you have a partner, maybe both of you can create divine genograms and explore your relational bonds. Contemplate for a moment the positive or negative ideas, feelings, thoughts, or patterns that have influenced your life. Where did they arise from? Were you unconsciously indoctrinated into a family and cultural field that shrouds some of your divine potential, health, and happiness? Do you have some unexplainable health problems? Or are there certain generational health issues that need more exploration? Are you plagued by caretaking responsibilities or suffering from an addiction? These are all questions that can be explored in your divine genogram and lead you to unravel the mystery of your divine qualities.

I extensively share my experience of working through family systems in my own life in *Blessings From a Thousand Generations*. I have also added a free workbook and fillable worksheets on my website (donnaevansstrauss.com) to help you uncover your heritage and unlock the keys to your divine genogram. This book and workbook guide you through a step-by-step process on how to make a genogram and track both the positive and negative love bonds from your ancestors.

Chapter 7:

How to Do a Genogram

The genogram was developed in the 1970s by Murray Bowen, a psychiatrist whom we talked about earlier in the chapter. His work focused on how family relationships and emotional patterns influence individual behavior across generations. Bowen's research emphasized that family dynamics play a critical role in shaping emotional and psychological well-being, and he believed we could use the genogram to achieve this.

Later, in the 1980s, Monica McGoldrick and Randy Gerson expanded on Bowen's ideas and formalized the genogram as a clinical tool for therapists. With the wisdom we also talked about in earlier chapters, we are going to further modify the tool so it covers all the different aspects. We will refine its structure but keep using the standardized symbols from McGoldrick et al. (1999), while expanding its application in psychotherapy, social work, and healthcare. Genograms have been widely used in family therapy, trauma counseling, and the medical field to track hereditary diseases and psychological patterns.

Traditionally, a genogram is a psychological tool used to map out family relationships, patterns, and dynamics across multiple generations. I invite you to see it as more than that for this section. To better understand this added perspective, imagine you are looking at prints in the sand or in the snow. Even if the people who left those prints are no longer there, you can get a good idea of how many they were, what ages they were, even gender and height, just from looking at the prints they left. The prints are an effect of something you would not have seen with your own eyes, but they are a very reliable pointer to what happened. In the same way, we can't always see into the A field, or understand the energy field of the family we are born into. We can, however, look at the prints the family members left in the sand and use that to understand the family's energy field.

The methods we will use go beyond a traditional family tree by incorporating emotional connections, behavioral patterns, and significant life events. This will be similar to how genograms are used in therapy and counseling, where they help individuals and professionals understand how family history influences psychological well-being, relationships, and even health conditions.

The negative and positive love bonds we have been talking about can be traced back through our lineage. In doing this, we can start a process of healing that resolves the negative love bonds, promotes the positive ones, and eventually brings to manifestation the divine qualities that God has set for you. To start this process, creating your own genogram will help you identify both positive and negative generational patterns. This process helps you uncover the mystery of the divine light that is hidden within these entangled family patterns.

Nature has a way of mirroring our journey back to us. If we contemplate for a moment how a tree grows from just a seed, within the seed is all the potential and divine design of the tree. The same is true for you, at the time of incarnation, your light is a seedpod of divinity that interpenetrates the earthplane and 127 into your parental DNA history. When a tree trunk is cut, you can see the amazing circles of life embedded or written into the fabric of the tree. Depending on the weather, the soil, and many other environmental factors, the tree is able to thrive, or parts of the tree thrive while others may not. You can see this when some branches seem to be withered.

This is the same as you incarnate into your family tree, or family mind field. The environmental field has a direct impact on how you grow and thrive. The environmental, family, cultural, and national lineage is interwoven into the very fabric of your consciousness. These fields of consciousness express or transmit both the positive and negative or dualistic experiences for you to navigate. In that process, inevitably, one or more of your divine qualities can become entangled with a negative love bond.

When we explore these events and honor our heritage, we can delve deeper than the trauma and find the alchemical presence of transfigurative love, grace, harmony, and infinite intelligence that guides us toward healing and unification. Simply put, all of the light within you has access to the infinite intelligent universe, infinite love, and infinite probabilities. When you access the depths of your core to transform or transfigure unhealthy patterns, you access seven main divine qualities that help you restore the interconnection between your core essence, the hara dimension, through the network of the chakra system, and into your human energy consciousness field. Inevitably, on a quantum level, every cell of your physical body begins to radiate and transmit frequencies of light from your core.

By adapting the traditional genogram tools, we can map out all of the different configurations within our family, reaching back several generations. We can explore all types of both healthy and unhealthy patterns. In 2011, when I wrote the first edition of Blessings from a Thousand Generations, I had a new revelation of how both the positive and negative love bonds in the family were actually offering us keys to unveil our journey home to our true selves or divine nature. The Old Testament offered us Ten Keys, hidden within the Ten Commandments, on how to awaken and reclaim the light within. These keys, when used in meditation, awaken the Merkaba form or Star of David light body within each 128 of us. Scripture invites us to write these on our hearts, souls, hands, and frontlet of our eyes.

> "6 These commandments that I give you today are to be on your hearts. 7 Impress them on your children. Talk about them when you sit at home and when you walk along the road, when you lie down and when you get up. 8 Tie them as symbols on your hands and bind them on your foreheads. 9 Write them on the doorframes of your houses and on your gates." (Det 6:6-9)

Meditating on these keys opens our communion with the light within us. Later in the Gospels, Christ directs us toward the inward journey when he says:

> "I and the Father are one." (John 10:30)

This is why it is important to unravel the mystery of the seven main divine qualities to awaken the unified transmission of consciousness from within you. Later, in Chapter eight, we will reflect on how trauma shrouds the human energy field and becomes entangled in unhealthy patterns. Then, in Chapter nine, we will explore how to access the divine qualities hidden within these patterns. You will learn how to transfigure or transmute these negative love bonds into the original expression of light and blessings. Remember you came as a blessing to this world, and it is within your innate power to radiate those blessings here, now.

Setting Up Your Genogram

McGoldrick et al (1999) share some symbols that have now been standardized for creating Genograms. These symbols represent everything from people to relationship types, whether they are still living or not, while showing where they place in your family tree. On the next page, in Figure 12, are the symbols that you can use to create and study your own genogram.

As I note in *Blessings from a Thousand Generations* first edition (Strauss, 2011):

> "Relationships between people are complex. These complexities can be charted by using some of the following symbols. The symbols help you identify patterns of a

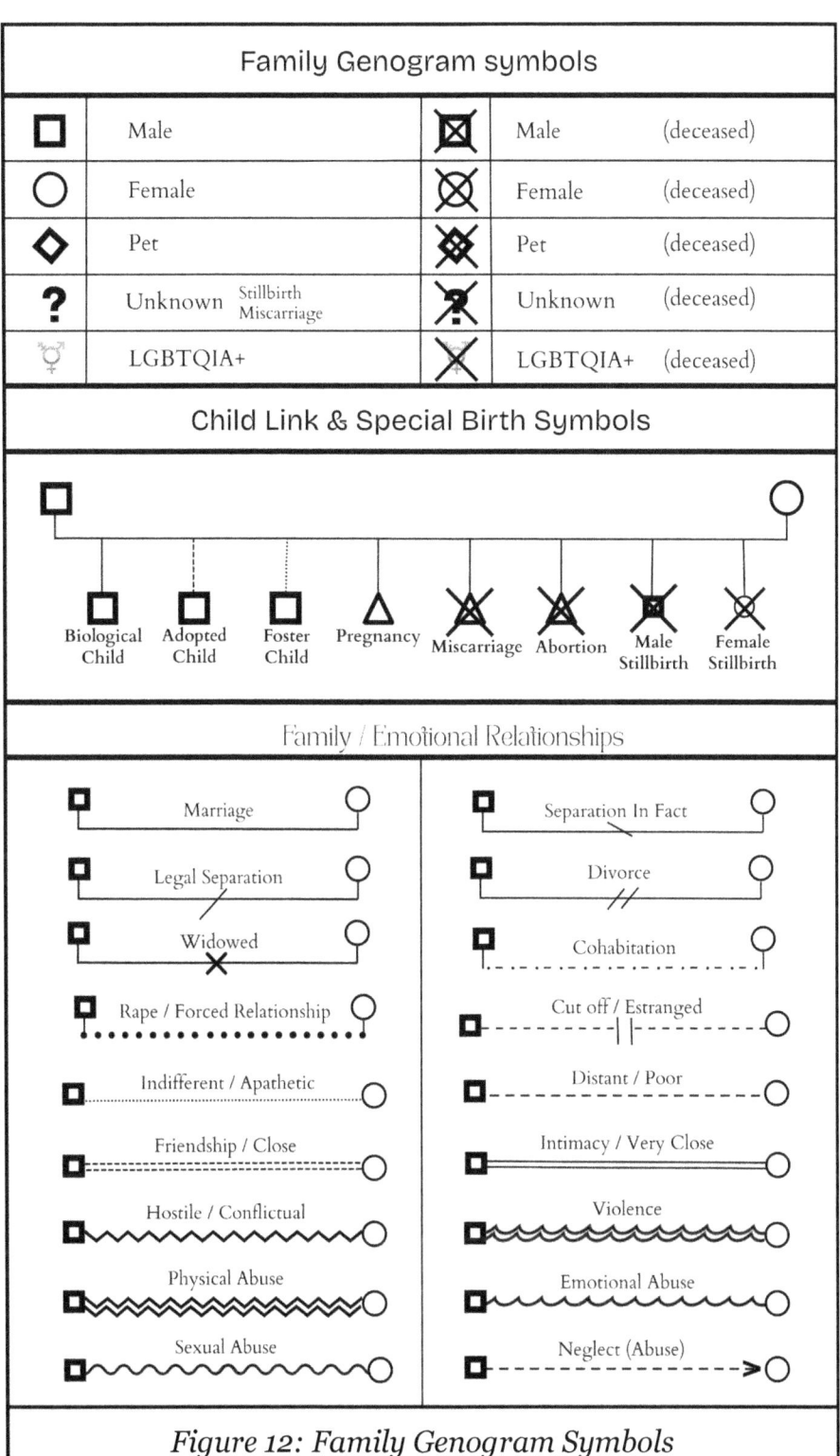

Figure 12: Family Genogram Symbols

healthy relationship between people and other issues that may signify a negative love bond pattern, such as divorce, living arrangements, estrangement, abuse, abandonment, adoptions, and isolation, and so on. Locate the symbols that best represent the relationships between people. Use the chart below to help simplify the process (pg. 22)."

Let us look at a step-by-step guide on how to create your Family Genogram. We start by making the Family Genogram Chart using the symbols in Figure 12 and following the questionnaire in Figure 13. I will use an example for the questionnaire so you can follow along.

We will be using the journey of CB (these are her initials to keep her information confidential) as our example, looking at how she has used the steps to create her Divine Genogram and understand her positive and negative love bonds. You can then create your own Genogram by recreating the questionnaire in your journal or by downloading the forms directly from my website, www.donnaevansstrauss.com.

Step 1: Gather Basic Family Information

Begin by documenting essential family details, including parents, children, grandparents, aunts, and uncles. Collect names, birthdates, and significant life events to create a foundational structure. CB created a family tree that had her relatives and information about the connections as shown on the next page.

Family Information Form
By: Donna Evans Strauss

FULL NAME: CB

BIRTH DATE: 04-10-1967

WAS THERE ADOPTION? Yes

NUMBER OF MARRIAGES: 1 (20 yrs) **NUMBER OF DIVORCES:** none

RELIGIOUS AFFILIATION: ex-Catholic **CULTURAL AFFILIATION:** Irish

MEDICAL HISTORY

DIAGNOSIS: Strep throat

PERIOD: Recurring until 2015

EFFECTS ON THE FAMILY: Contagion | Absence from school

MENTAL HEALTH HISTORY

DIAGNOSIS: PTSD/Addiction / suicide ideation/

PERIOD: MULTIPLE TIMES SINCE AGE 9

EFFECTS ON THE FAMILY: SEPARATION DUE TO OBSESSION WITH DRUGS | OVERDOSE AT AGE 21

POSITIVE LOVE BONDS
Positive Beliefs and Patterns

COMPASSIONATE | LOVING (DAD +GM) | GENEROUS | KIND | WISE | (G) | THE GOLDEN RULE | TOLERANT (GM)

NEGATIVE LOVE BONDS
Negative Beliefs and Patterns

AVOIDANCE (DAD +MOM) | CARETAKING (GM) | SUBMISSION (DAD + GM) | NEGATIVITY (MOM +GF) | SEXUALITY | CONTROLLING | LOVE

MAIN EMOTIONAL COLORINGS

SADNESS | GRIEF | SENSE OF ABANDONMENT | REJECTION | SENSITIVITY | DEPRESSION | ANXIETY | PTSD SYMPTOMS | SHAME | SUICIDE IDEATION

FEARS

ABANDONMENT | REJECTION | VIOLENCE | UNLOVABLE | HUMILIATION (MOM+GF+DAD)

ADDITIONAL COMMENTS

Figure 13: The Family Information Form

Step 2: Map Out Relationships

The next step is to map out the relationships from both your paternal and maternal families. For this example, I will use my own charts to protect the identity of CB. These examples are from Blessings From a Thousand Generations. Following my example, you can map the relationships between everyone in your own family. As you fill this form out, identify patterns of closeness, distance, conflict, or support within the family unit.

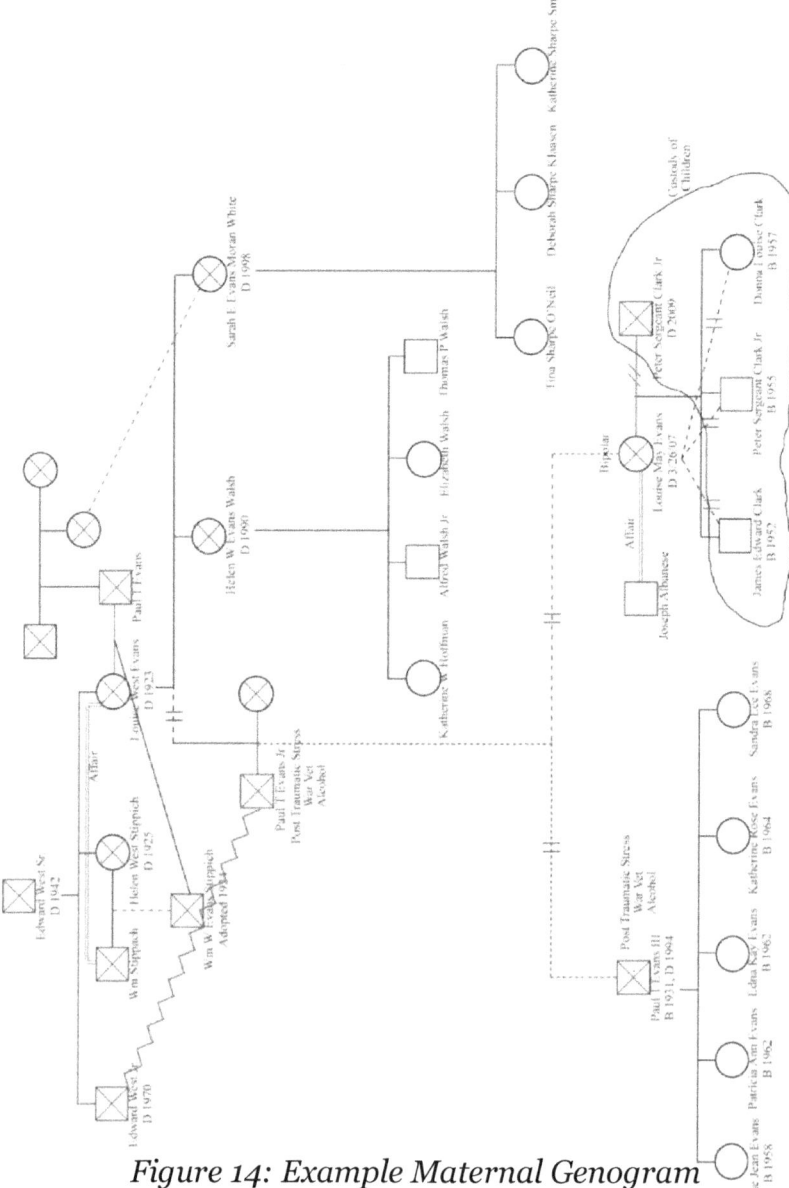

Figure 14: Example Maternal Genogram

Step 3: Identify Relationship Issues

On your chart, note key relationship dynamics—such as estrangements, conflicts, or strong emotional bonds—that have shaped family interactions over time. In addition, also map psychological conditions such as depression, anxiety, PTSD, or addiction. Record major health conditions like heart disease, diabetes, dementia, or pregnancy-related issues such as miscarriages. Examine how these medical histories have impacted the family, including hospitalizations, caregiver stress, or emotional strain.

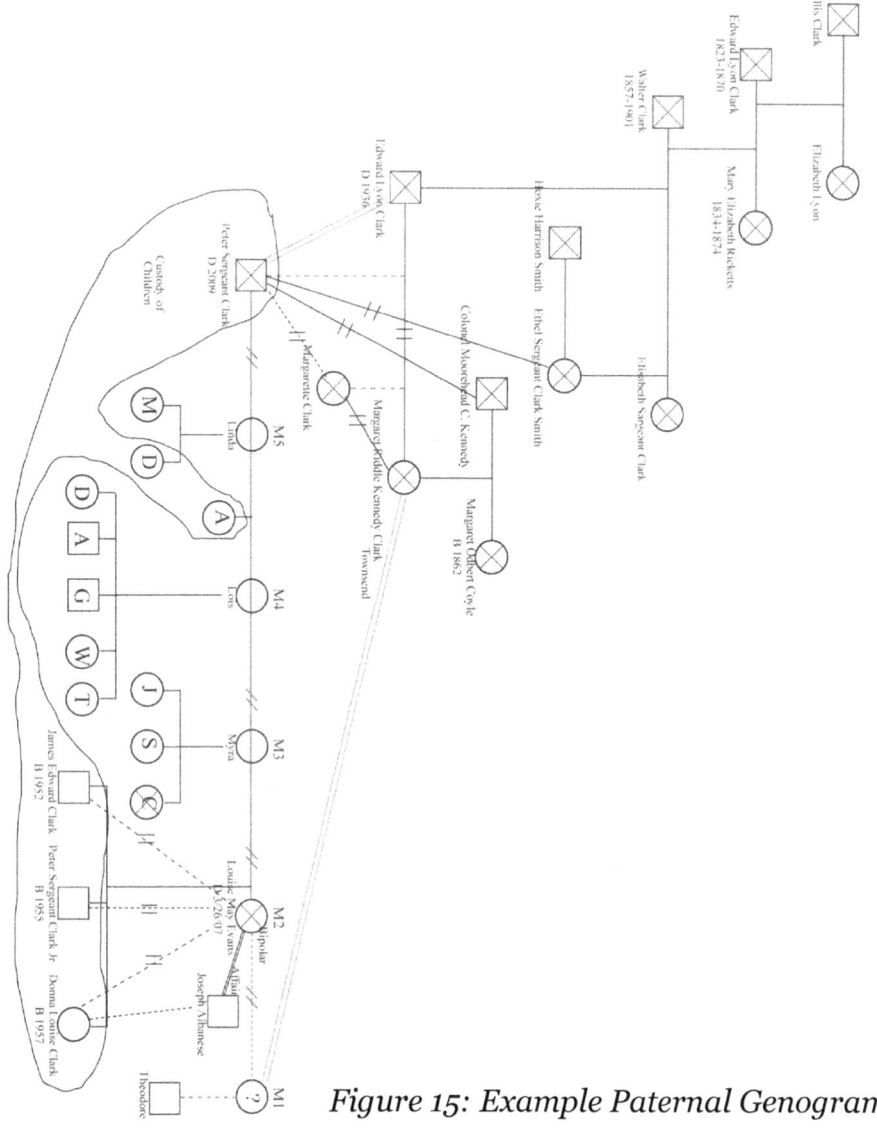

Figure 15: Example Paternal Genogram

Step 4: Recognize Family Beliefs

CB completed this process by comprehensively studying her family beliefs through journaling. Below are some of the entries from her journals. In your journal, identify core beliefs—both positive and negative—that influence generational patterns of love and relationships. For example, experiences of abandonment may lead to beliefs of unworthiness or mistrust.

Identify recurring emotional patterns in the family, such as anger, sadness, fear, shame, or joy.

Look for major fears within the family, such as fear of abandonment, authority, or losing control. Consider how these fears shape behavior and decision-making across generations. Start by focusing on one or two dominant emotions that appear across generations.

Identify moments where family members lost their sense of spiritual connection or inheritance, whether through personal choices, external circumstances, or generational shifts in values.

Reflect on how negative generational patterns relate to deeper spiritual principles, such as trust, forgiveness, and personal healing. You can trace the ten spiritual keys and see how they might have been violated in the past by some family members.

Later, you will chart how these beliefs have been passed down.

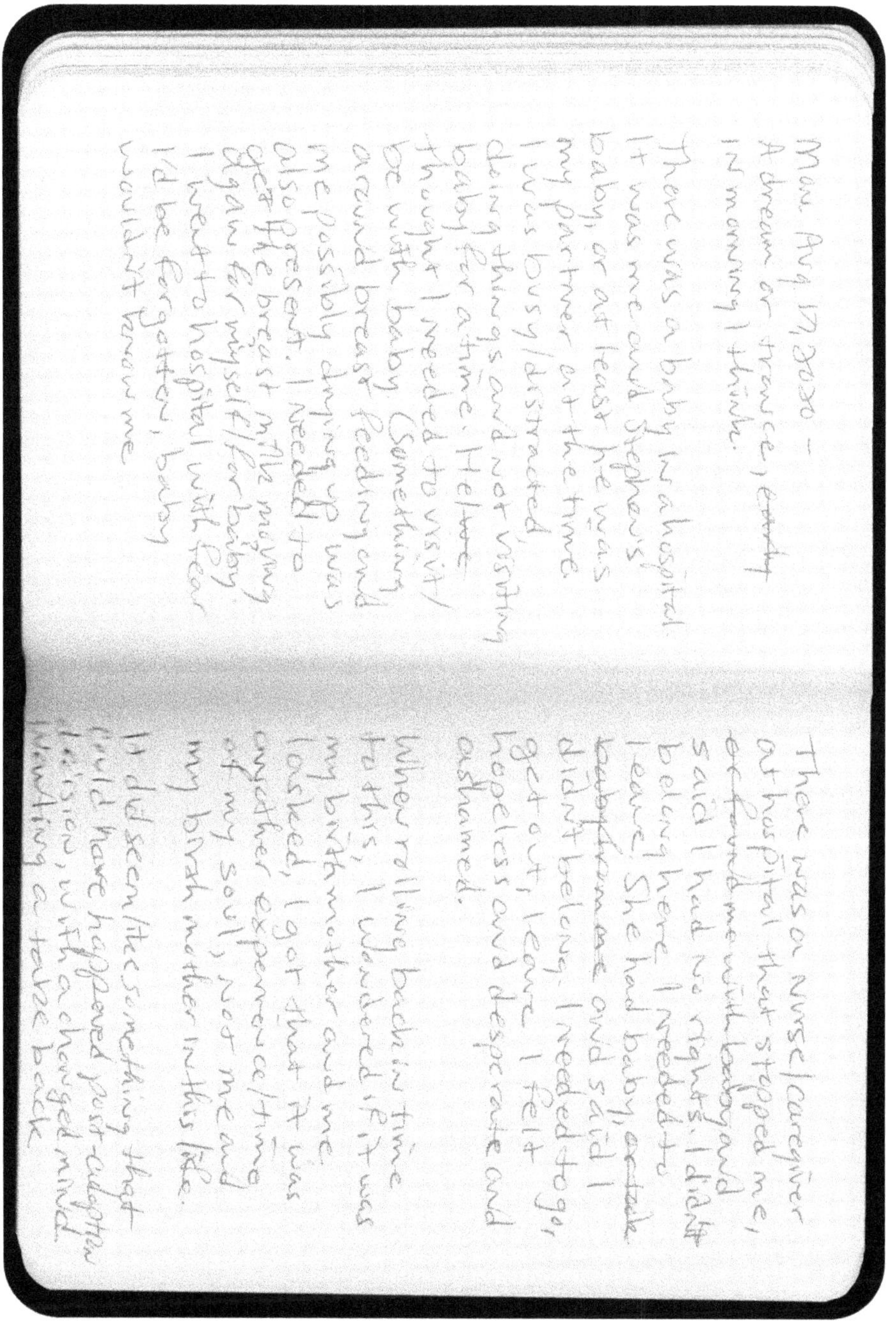

Mon. Aug 17, 2020 –
A dream or trance, early
in morning I think.

There was a baby in a hospital.
It was me and Stephen's
baby, or at least he was
my partner at the time.
I was busy/distracted,
doing things and not visiting
baby for a time. He was
thought I needed to visit/
be with baby. Something
around breast feeding and
me possibly drying up was
also present. I needed to
get the breast milk moving
again for myself/for baby.
I went to hospital with fear
I'd be forgotten, baby
wouldn't know me.

There was a nurse/caregiver
at hospital that stopped me,
or found me with baby and
said I had no rights. I didn't
belong here. I needed to
leave. She had baby, or took
baby from me and said I
didn't belong. I needed to go,
get out, leave. I felt
hopeless and desperate and
ashamed.

When rolling back in time
to this, I wondered if it was
my birth mother and me
(asked). I got that it was
another experience/time
of my soul, not me and
my birth mother in this life.

It did seem like something that
could have happened post-adoption
decision, with a changed mind,
wanting a take back

Figure 16: Example From CB's Journal

Step 5: Connect Patterns to Spiritual Insights

Reflect on how negative generational patterns relate to deeper spiritual principles, such as trust, forgiveness, and personal healing. You can trace the ten spiritual keys and see how they might have been violated in the past by some family members.

Bring all the insight from the previous steps and populate your genogram. Below, I have shared a real-life example from one of my female clients, CB, whom we have been following through the example. Her life, while different from yours, can help you to draw parallels as you work on your own genogram. CB was adopted at birth and explores her challenges by examining her genogram.

Her reflection on the form below highlights issues with rejection sensitivity, feelings of belonging, and being mirrored for her authentic gifts, experiences, and insights. Working with the divine genogram helped identify both the positive and negative love bonds, faulty assumptions, and suppressed divine qualities (these are covered in the last chapter). Although these painful events occurred, CB could reclaim her light and release the transgenerational patterns from both her birth parents and adoptive parents. Through self-discovery and healing, she found her true self anchored in transfiguration.

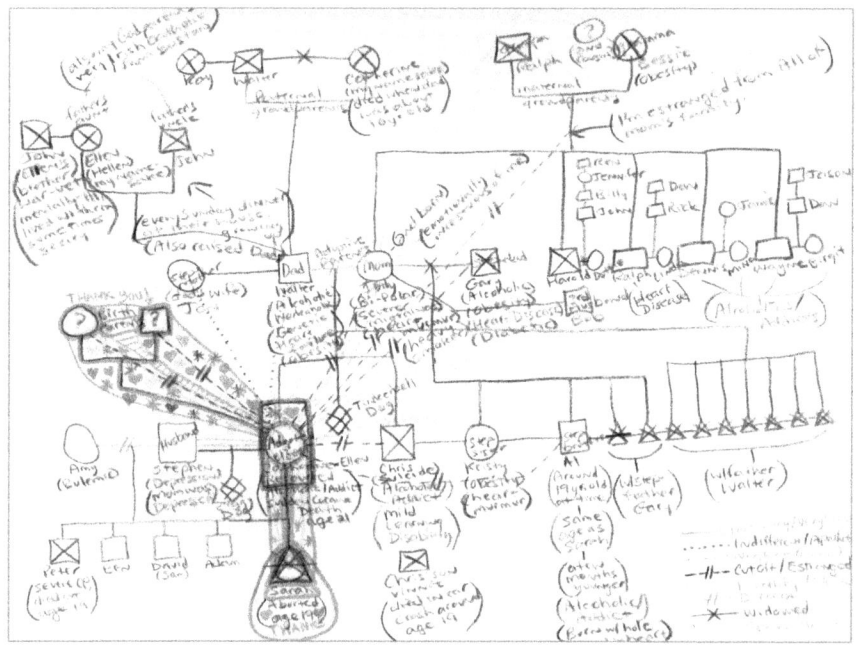

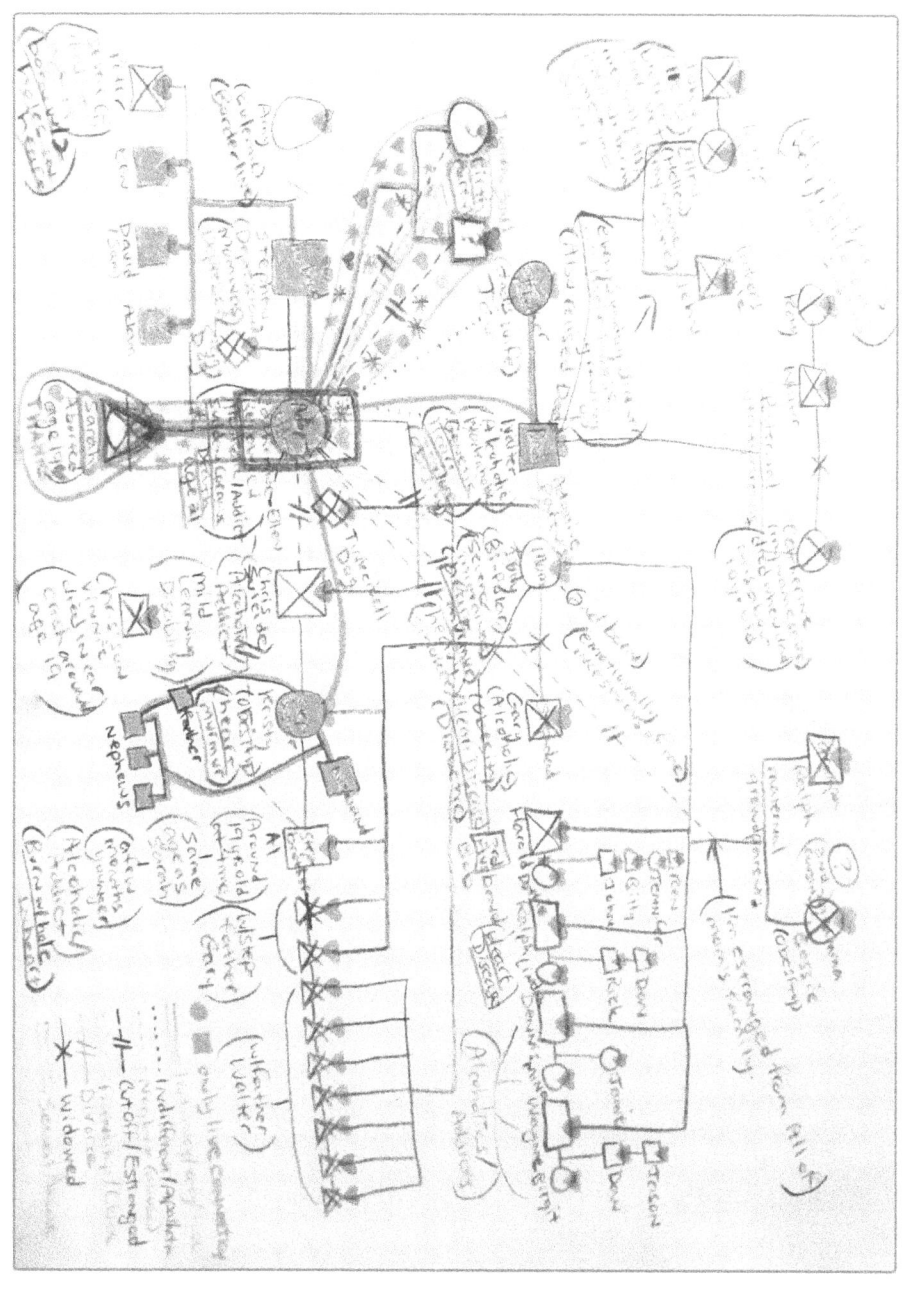

Figure 17: Example of CB's Family Genogram (More Details)

The Genogram, Trauma, & Divine Qualities

By integrating the knowledge from your personal genogram, identifying your personal negative love bonds and trauma, you can reveal the suppressed divine qualities within. When we recognize that trauma can bond with light and love, the energy and consciousness can become frozen in time, trapped in a cycle of repeated patterns. When you explore the seven divine qualities: Divine Trust, Divine Love and Acceptance, Divine Respect, Divine Relationships, Divine Communication, Divine Vision, and Divine Wisdom.

You fully understand that as an incoming soul and infant, you bring these blessings of light into the world to illuminate the darkness and help your family and society to remember the truth of their cosmic origins. The patterns you are born into are a family, cultural, religious, and societal mind field. There are multidimensional waves of pure love, joy, and communion, as well as these energies becoming entangled within the process of becoming human. We naturally engage and adapt to these fields of consciousness.

I invite you to now identify which divine qualities were suppressed in your family. You can use the mantras in Chapter nine to change the embedded patterns that stop the flow of the quality to reach its full expression and potential. All these qualities reside within as true potential and expression of the blessings you incarnated to radiate into the world. Each quality has the potential to transmute or transfigure the transgenerational love bonds and restore your innate nature, health, and wellbeing.

The next chapter explores the different types of trauma and their impact on you and your human biofield. This chapter will give you insight into the different chakras and levels of your energy field. Trauma has an impact on each level of our expression, from feeling safe in the world to expressing our real needs, our sense of belonging, and feeling loved. By exploring these levels and the divine qualities, we can bring coherence from the core of our being to reclaim our true nature and experience ourselves as being blessed and as a blessing to our family and the world.

Chapter 8:

Trauma Perspectives

Imagine looking at yourself through a cracked, dirty mirror—or maybe a kaleidoscope where all the images change and fold in upon each other, and where some of the facets are beautiful and clear while others are occluded by colliding forces of two polarities. What you see is a distorted representation of who you are. You will see dirt where there isn't any, and your face might seem disfigured when it is not. Many people go through life never seeing their true potential, adopting a distorted view of themselves.

Over the past 40 years, we have seen the advent of ancestry research on the internet and an increase in television programs exploring our ancestral roots. These sites have inspired the curiosity and exploration of so many people. I believe these explorations have a deeper meaning and are clues to answering the very basic questions: "Who am I? Where did I come from? What am I?"

Coinciding with this excitement is the reality of possibly revealing a traumatic history. Unraveling these stories is like the process of finding rare gems, where you need to dig through layers of pain, sorrow, unhealthy belief systems, and social and cultural biases to reach the treasure. Like an archaeologist, we can unravel these transgenerational stories and some of the positive and painful history that may impact how we perceive ourselves. Digging through the past can be challenging, yet there is always a greater mystery within the buried treasure chest. The radiance of our core reveals itself—just as a rare gem sparkles through the dirt, our light radiates from our core. Reconciling the history of our maternal and paternal ancestors offers us the opportunity to become free, healthy, and happy.

My journey wasn't an easy one, and it was more painful to uncover some stories than others. Yet, going through these entangled narratives opened a pathway for me to embrace my confusion and suffering and claim my true birthright. I am born of cosmic light and am free to express all of these divine qualities. My hope is that these insights and practices will guide you deeper on your journey. If we walk together through the fire, untangle the negative love bonds, and uncover our true selves, our love and light will radiate forth. We will reclaim our true destiny and experience the light emerging from within.

In my 35 years of teaching and working with students and clients, I have found it invaluable to use the practices in this book to guide them on their journey. Each step of a person's journey is important. The first is ensuring their commitment to the transformation process, and that they have the curiosity and determination to explore their history and uncover painful memories. This part can take time, and some people need more time than others. Transformation brings us insights and discovery, while transcendence expands our view and releases us from our limited self-definitions. Transfiguration or transmutation occurs when our distorted self-definition dissolves, our unresolved emotions are integrated, and our divine qualities are free to emanate from within.

It's okay to step back for a moment if you need to. Some students reported reading *Hands of Light* over 20 years ago and only now feeling ready to enter the School. Also, this process doesn't require you to enter a school; it only requires your commitment to your journey. The next steps may seem simple, or you may say, "Why bother? I know this in my head already." I encourage you to start the process and use the fillable templates on my website (donnaevansstrauss.com) to help guide you along the way. Remember, the divine genogram process is about reclaiming your true self.

By taking this journey, you may be surprised to find inner qualities that bring new meaning to your life. You can start today by empowering yourself with the practices within these pages. By unraveling the mystery hidden beneath your memories, you will find your authentic self and purpose in life. Your intention to find meaning activates your higher self, which transmits divine wisdom, divine love, and the divine matrix to untangle the negative love bonds and frozen memories that hold you hostage to the past. Sometimes, I am known to say, "Why is the past stealing the present moment of the now?"

Divine wisdom is emanating from you, flowing from the infinite universe and informing your rational mind. You can release the negative love bond patterns and free the transfigurative love and grace that emerge from deep within your core. Transfigurative love transmutes the unhealthy beliefs, emotions, and behaviors into pure radiated love. Uncovering those golden gems—the divine qualities within—allows your cosmic consciousness to flow freely.

It's like when Christ said in Matthew 5:15–16 (*Holy Bible, New International Version*, 2013/1973):

> Neither do people light a lamp and put it under a bowl. Instead, they put it on its stand, and it gives light to everyone in the house. In the same way, let your light shine before others, that they may see your good deeds and glorify your Father in Heaven.

You were born of light, and you can reclaim your birthright. To truly be born again is to remember the light within you. It has always been there, awaiting your self-discovery. You only need to remember.

In the previous chapter, we explored how your divinity can be suppressed or hidden beneath a shroud of confusion, painful experiences, and transgenerational negative love bonds. Exploring the entangled past of our ancestors has a direct impact on our evolution and our ability to reclaim the truth of the emerging light from within. Our families create a familial mind field to which we adapt as we grow. The unhealed emotional and cognitive pollution from the past creates an invisible field that impacts our subconscious and acts like a computer program that informs our responses.

Remember when we talked about the seven challenges as spheres of consciousness that emanate around the Earth? The unhealthy and unresolved transmissions within the A-field emanate from the Earth's morphogenetic field. We incarnate through these lower spheres of consciousness to bring blessings of light, wisdom, and love. You can imagine this field of family trauma in the same way—it can appear like spheres of consciousness emanating from the Earth, and you are born into these spheres of consciousness. Depending on your intention and your soul's longing to be light and blessings, you select certain patterns to help illuminate and heal. Next, let's explore how trauma impacts the human biofield.

Trauma & the Human Biofield

Over the past couple of chapters, we have explored a new paradigm, shifting our perceptions from a world based in solid matter to one that is informed and formed by frequencies of energy and consciousness. We have proposed seven stages of how our light incarnates through the four dimensions, the final one being the physical body. On the opposite spectrum, the core star dimension expands our perceptual reality beyond our natural experiences. Deep down, though, we are connected to a reality that is far beyond natural experience. Knowing this, we can now look at trauma, disease, and negative love bonds from a different perspective. Since we have multiple dimensions to our existence, it follows that trauma affects us differently across those dimensions.

To start with, let's look at what trauma is. According to the Centre for Addiction and Mental Health (n.d.):

Trauma is the lasting emotional response that often results from living through a distressing event. Experiencing a traumatic event can harm a person's sense of safety, sense of self, and ability to regulate emotions and navigate relationships. Long after the traumatic event occurs, people with trauma can often feel shame, helplessness, powerlessness, and intense fear. (para 1)

Trauma is very hard to define, though, because it not only affects your physical body but also ripples through your entire being and impacts your deep limbic system, nervous system, and other bodily systems. Trauma impacts us at the physical, emotional, psychological, relational, social, and spiritual level. I want you to think of trauma as a wave that runs throughout your entire being and leaves imprints that affect who you are and how you see yourself.

These imprints and impressions reside deep within your human energy biofield and eventually impact your health and happiness. Understanding the fundamental truth that Christ taught—do not hide your light under a bushel—confirms the importance of going through these traumas to unravel the mystery of the light within you. The divine genogram offers you an opportunity to explore these traumatic events with one main goal in mind: to lift the shroud of these traumatic experiences so you can authentically experience your divine birthright. The light that is entangled in unresolved conflicts, distorted images, and blocked emotions becomes free, and you can then express your creativity, love, light, and wisdom.

The key resides in your perceptual reality. Your persona or self-identity orients you toward an outer focused sense of self. Reorienting toward your core will awaken a new understanding of your divine birthright. Working with your divine genogram offers you a step-by-step self-empowerment process that reconciles the past while restoring each of your divine qualities.

Let's explore the impact of trauma on the seven levels of the human energy consciousness field (HECF) from the Brennan

Healing Science model; Barbara Brennan called it the human energy consciousness system (HECS). So, when you go through a traumatic experience, it affects you at all levels of your HECF and hara, except the core light. In *Core Light Healing*, Brennan (2017) introduces the concept that our traumas are held within the HECS, when the core light curls in on itself. From my perspective, it contracts just like holding your breath. In that contraction, on the hara dimension you shift your intention toward survival, while in the human biofield you store held emotions, assumptions, and misconceptions about yourself, others, and the world. Remember that each dimension of your being arises from your core dimension.

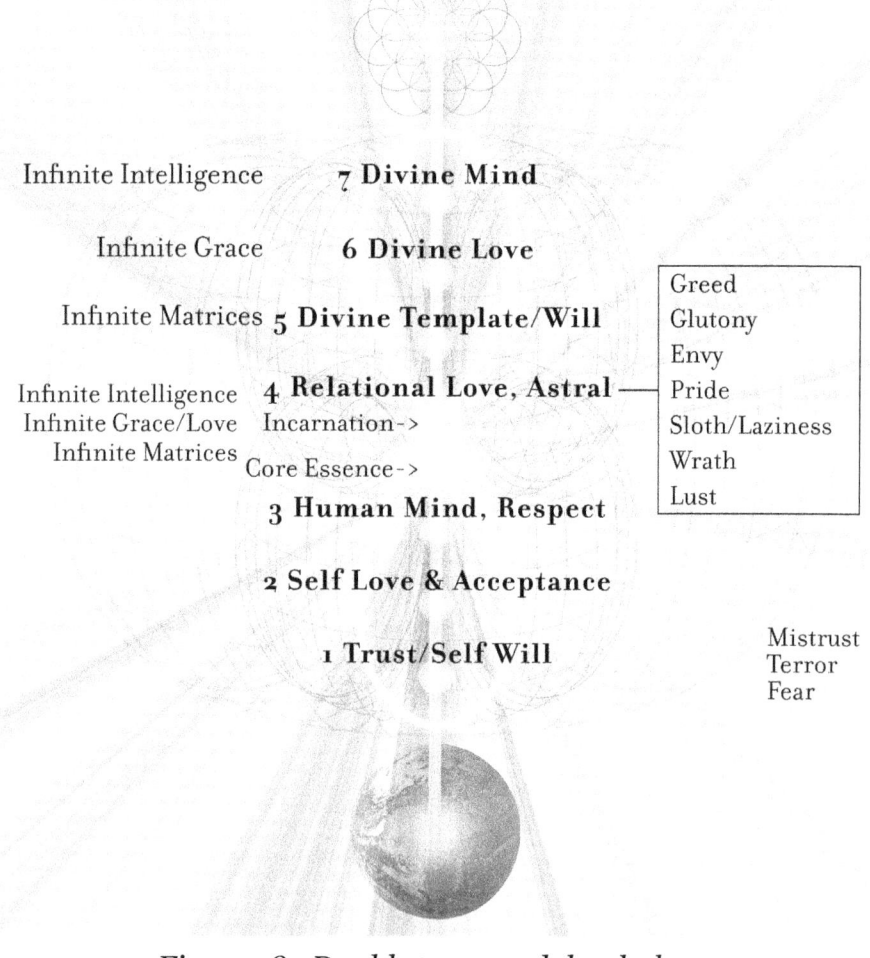

Figure 18 : Double torus and the chakras

So, when you have a prolonged contraction from trauma, your core energy pulls inward in a contraction and tries to find a solution to navigate the tension or danger. In modern psychology, these solutions have many names, from defenses to habits, addictions, depression, and psychological disorders. You are supposed to be the expression of the core light in the world, but when you are affected by trauma, the path of the light becomes entangled. This is like having a basket or shroud of unhealthy consciousness over your light.

Let's explore how trauma impacts the seven levels of the human biofield. The layers of the human biofield are like holographic spheres of consciousness that appear as blankets; they are also interpenetrating frequencies of light transmitting information from the core. These layers extend from your chakra system outward, as shown in Figure 18. According to Barbara Brennan in Light Emerging (Brennan, 2011b), there are seven layers to our aura, just as there are seven chakras in our human biofield. Let's have a brief overview of these layers and how they are affected by trauma.

Trauma at the Seventh Level & Seventh Chakra

The seventh level is the divine mind, the universal mind. It emerges from the core or infinite intelligent universe, which many of us are accustomed to calling God, the I AM, Brahman, Allah, Great Spirit, Buddha, and other names. In the Old Testament, it is stated that we are made in the image of God. Most of us consider this to be literal—that our physical bodies are made in the image and likeness of God. But perhaps it is our cosmic bodies, our core essence, our hara, and our HECF that are reflected in the human form that represents God's likeness. Each level of our field represents a holographic aspect of God.

The seventh level looks like a golden holographic grid structure that permeates every cell of your body and acts as the inner and outer shield to your human biofield. The infinite intelligent universe creates the matrix of the divine mind. The upper structured levels provide the matrix for the lower structured levels, just as the upper unstructured levels transmit the frequency and vibration to the lower unstructured levels.

As stated, the divine mind is a holographic replica of the infinite intelligent universe. It connects us to the invisible world of the cosmos and universal consciousness. The access point is through the human biofield, where the windows of light or seals of the seven chakras transmit the frequencies that form the seventh level.

As you review the double torus (Figure 18), you will notice that the holographic pattern repeats itself on the lower third level, which represents the human mind and is a holographic structured level that is imprinted with all the learned knowledge from incarnation to the present. The third level has access to the wisdom and insight of the seventh level through meditation practices. This is where unknown solutions to problems synchronize and quicken your awareness. It is like tapping into universal consciousness and downloading new information.

But as a child, your third level has to develop here on Earth from that template of the seventh level and engage through the developmental stages of learning. Sometimes, you will forget your connection to the divine mind, only to reconnect now and then when you have revelations or epiphanies. You can develop the capacity to access this level of consciousness through meditation and intuition practices that are designed to open a clear transmission. Some people have access to direct knowing as one of the awakened sensory perceptions.

This has probably happened to you—maybe you've been working on a problem and you can't think of a solution, so you take a walk in the park and, all of a sudden, the answer comes out of this universal divine mind. You pressed your consciousness into the infinite intelligent field while surrendering your ego, and in that quiet moment, all of a sudden you received a download of new information.

It does not come only to you, though; the answer is released into the morphogenetic sphere because, most likely, there will be a thousand people asking that same question. So, when you are going to create something but someone else does so first, and you think, *Oh my, I thought of that too—they stole my idea*, it's not always like that. Remember the experiment with rats and the morphogenetic field we went over earlier? Humans are like that too. Once knowledge of something has been released into the field, we all have the answer.

Your role is to bring the idea back through the developmental stages and into manifestation on the earthly plane—and this is what the challenge often is, because doing so takes focus, passion, integration, and work. This is where the seventh chakra and the front and rear aspects of the sixth chakra come together. The idea needs to come into form and steps need to be taken for this to happen. If the rear aspect of the sixth chakra is blocked, you may lose interest before you see your ideas come to fruition.

Here, you may need to hire someone skilled in knowing how to take each step to bring an idea into form. This happens in business all the time—you need a visionary, and you also need people with very practical skills who love working on details and all the stages and steps of a project. Teams are great because everyone brings in their gifts and supports each other.

We are always being imprinted with new ideas that we can manifest. What happens is we take the idea and create a plan to bring it to fruition. Here, the seventh level works with the practical aspect of the third level, the human mind; we will explore this aspect later. We follow the steps to manifest the idea, riding the creative wave, which is the light coming in through the creative idea. We then learn to solidify that idea by organizing it, which is akin to setting goals toward achieving everything. This takes place during children's development as well. When we were kids, everything seemed like a great idea, but as we grew up, we solidified that way of thinking into guiding principles and a specific frame of mind.

Sometimes people get an influx of ideas, but they don't know how to take the steps to integrate and solidify them, or they're blocked from communicating them, so they don't achieve their goal. The full wave of the idea has to come through the whole human plane of creativity and communication until it's structured and made manifest. This interweaves with the sixth level, which we are going to look at next.

Trauma at the Sixth Level & Sixth Chakra

The core essence emanates through the seals of the chakras on the sixth level as infinite grace and transfigurative love. Emerging from the center of the universe and your core is the power to alchemically change anything in your life through access to and transmission of this purest frequency of love and grace. This transmission is so powerful that it illuminates your sixth level with spiritual ecstasy. Think of the grace and transfigurative love transmitting into the Earth plane on the sixth level, and its frequency changes to divine love and ecstasy.

There is a Scripture in Ephesians 2:4–9 that defines grace very well (*Holy Bible, New International Version*, 2013/1973):

> But because of his great love for us, God, who is rich in mercy, made us alive with Christ even when we were dead in transgressions—it is by grace you have been saved. And God raised us with Christ and seated us with him in the heavenly realms in Christ Jesus so that in the coming ages he might show the incomparable riches of his grace, expressed in his kindness to us in Christ Jesus. For it is by grace you have been saved, through faith—and this not from yourselves, it is the gift of God—not by works, so that no one can boast.

So, it is through grace that we have a divine genome within us. It is not something we earn by doing something, nor something that is for a select few only. No, grace is the divine enablement, making it possible for us to experience the bliss of our core while living through this human experience.

Imagine for a moment the highest frequency of love and grace transmitting from your core through the holographic human biofield on the sixth level. The frequencies of transmission change when entering the human biofield through this level. On the sixth level, grace and transfigurative love—God's unmerited favor—radiate and permeate our profound forgetting.

Universal and transfigurative love transmits into your life, and these transmissions change frequently as they enter the human biofield. On the sixth level, we experience divine ecstasy, like standing on a mountaintop and feeling the majestic nature of the universe and Earth—or perhaps like the moment you met your partner and there was a spark of jubilation. At other times when you are suffering or feeling a sense of being lost, a guiding presence or light might lift you out of the darkness and set you back on your path.

When we experience traumatic events on an earthly level, we begin to block or doubt this flow of grace and light. When we enter the fourth level on the earthly plane of human relationships, our negative and positive experiences respectively block and allow the flow of love that unites us with others. If we experience heartbreak, loss, and discouragement and leave them unattended, we block the flow of grace and love into our lives.

In doing so, we hold onto painful images, feelings, and defenses that shift or contract the natural flow of light into the world. On the sixth level of the field, this blocked energy may appear as clouds or murkiness around a particular chakra on the sixth level. The chakra will indicate the type of blockage, such as a broken heart, fear of our expression of sensuality, or an inability to see the light in others, to name a few.

When divine love subscends into the earthly plane, moving into the fourth level of the relationship, the frequency changes and it is expressed as human love. It will continue to change even further into the second level, where it is expressed as self-love and acceptance. An interference in this transmission can obstruct its flow and frequency.

What you need to remember is that it is one love—infinite grace transmitting from the core into the Earth plane by opening the seals of the chakras on each level. We do not make more love; rather, we open its unending flow, which emerges from the core of our being. Here, love can be bonded in positive or negative ways.

You probably wonder why you keep repeating some of your negative patterns even though you do not want to. It is because they are anchored in your subconscious field. Unearthing how love was bonded in their family can be challenging for some. On an irrational level, it feels like giving up the pattern would be like giving up one of our parents. However, if we recognize that we may not know how to create a positive love bond, letting go can be a courageous act.

Our emotional bodies are very unstructured and colorful, just like the colors of a rainbow or the exquisite colors of the universe. The higher-level frequencies appear more opalescent, while the lower levels appear as the primary colors we see in a rainbow. When divine ecstasy is blocked on the sixth level, we experience a disconnect from our divine roots. Perhaps we doubt that God or infinite intelligence exists. We turn away from our spiritual roots.

Trauma at the Fifth Level & Fifth Chakra

The fifth level is the divine template—a blueprint—for the first level. It has within it everything written about every cell of your body. So, if you have any physical trauma, say you've cut your leg or damaged your liver, there will be a tear at the fifth level of the field as well that needs to be addressed. If someone has their kidney removed from their physical body, when they come for healing there will be entanglement at the fifth level that we need to address to bring healing to the rest of the body.

Imagine a computer running from a code that makes everything function well. When you damage the hardware of the computer, it affects the execution of that code, even for parts of the computer that are not damaged. Moving back to the body, energetically untangling the block in the fifth level can feed the first level even though the kidney has been removed.

When we experience developmental trauma at any stage, this chakra can become blocked. We may feel insecure in speaking up or communicating our ideas. Some people may even feel anxiety prior to speaking to others or in a group setting; this anxiety can feel overwhelming, and the fifth chakra closes. This chakra also regulates hearing and how we listen to others, how we learn, and how we take in and assimilate information. When someone experiences trauma, their brain and wiring may shut down in certain ways. You may feel frightened and not be able to hear a word someone is saying; you seem present, yet you realize that part of you left, contracted. Part of your consciousness energetically escaped. People oftentimes report these symptoms, and may be diagnosed with different types of disorders. Paying attention to these moments can bring great insights on how to integrate the divine qualities that will heal these patterns.

Healing on the First & Fifth Levels

The divine design of the morphogenetic field for our bodies exists in the fifth level as a template that is then holographically imprinted into the first level. So, every body part you have emanates from the divine template, whose perfect form is in the fifth level. For example, your liver's perfect template is there in the fifth level, but the hologram in the first level can become sick and need to be recalibrated to the divine template so it becomes healthy again. Imagine for a moment the eight billion livers on the planet and how many are functioning at the highest level of design. Your liver also communicates with all other livers within this matrix. I know this sounds way out there, but contemplate the fact that when several girls or women either live together or work together, their menstrual cycles become in sync. There is a communication transmitted through this invisible matrix or field of consciousness.

This is why and how energy healing works. Healers tap into the higher frequency of the fifth-level template of the field, repairing this level and realigning or calibrating the first level. So, if you are undergoing a liver transplant or have liver disease, the healer can transmit that higher-frequency energy into the fifth and the first level to create coherence and cohesion between the two. The first-level hologram of the liver starts to realign with the divine template in level five.

In addition, the fifth-level template relates to divine will, the divine plan, and holds the matrix for all sentient life. When we align our free will, which arises upon incarnation through our fourth level and chakra, with our self-will, which relates to the first chakra, our lives and life purpose align in an effortless flow. Imagine for a moment that you are in harmonic synchronicity with the divine design of your life's purpose. Your life becomes effortless in the flow. Now imagine pushing or feeding off the wave—how do your free will and self-will get activated? Consider the possibility that you have the power in any moment to connect with the divine flow of your life by aligning your self-will with free will, and ultimately with divine will. Breathe this awareness through you and find the effortless flow of your life's purpose.

Trauma on the Fourth Level & Fourth Chakra

The fourth chakra and level of the human biofield allows us to explore the bridge between two worlds: Heaven and Earth, above and below. In the double torus, you can see the heart chakra as the eye of the torus, the center point of the infinity sign. The spiritual worlds that are expressed in the upper spheres of consciousness directly correlate with incarnation from the core and hara dimensions into the fourth level and physical dimension of the Earth realm. When you look at the illustration of the double torus in Figure 18, you can see how the chakra system and vertical power current emerge from the core star and hara dimension interacting with the morphogenetic field of the Earth plane.

Let's now introduce the concept of how the human biofield forms. The upper levels of the double torus engage with the morphogenetic field or matrix of the Earth plane, and it is here that the lower portion of the double torus is transfigured by the human matrix. The perfect design of a human being is held in this Earth memory field. All sentient life on Earth has a matrix that is like a computer or memory program for its design; that is, life or matter that exists on this planet has a memory field.

If we've experienced any type of relational trauma, such as heartbreak, loss, devastation, or abuse, the transmission of radiance and divine love from the sixth level will become entangled, forming a negative love bond. The field and chakra can become murky, blocked with thick, unexpressed pain, sorrow, rage, and disappointment. People can experience heart pain, congestive heart problems, and breathing problems when navigating being in a relationship with others here on Earth. That's the elation of your core essence. When that core essence can transmit downward, it changes frequency. As your light—all that love—starts to come into the Earth, it starts to adjust to the frequency changes. That love gets changed and transfigured because we have all this hurt in our hearts that we have not dealt with. The high frequency of that love starts to get splintered off, bit by bit.

Let's explore how transgenerational trauma can be transmitted via collective spheres of consciousness formed around the Earth. Our feelings about ourselves and others can become entangled, where love is bonded in a negative and unhealthy way. Your innate gift of transfigurative love and grace subscends from the core through the sixth level, yet engages on the fourth level and finds a way to navigate being in human relationships that form either positive or negative love bonds. The love that becomes entangled and blocked from flowing forms a time capsule—a kind of frozen consciousness that holds memories and feelings from the developmental stage at which the entanglement or blockage occurred. If these types of events continue to happen, they build upon each other and eventually create physical, emotional, psychological, relational, and spiritual health challenges. The core star's transmission of love cannot pass these hurdles; instead, it curls in on itself and becomes suppressed at that level. The core star will always continue to exist, yet it cannot express its innate quality of relational love.

When the Flower of Life interpenetrates and interacts with the morphogenetic field of the Earth, activating the divine matrix, that is the template for our human form. When this is activated, the infinity sign shifts into a horizontal position and forms the double torus. The upper chakras and levels of the field correlate with the transmission of infinite intelligence, infinite grace, and infinite creative designs, while the frequencies of the upper spheres of consciousness transmit through the fourth level around the Earth plane, which holds the Akashic records of our Earth plane.

These records transmit the highest level of human and earthly consciousness as well as spheres of lower-level consciousness. The incoming soul transmigrating into the Earth plane intentionally moves through these spheres, passing through the lower-level spheres that hold the emotional and cognitive pollution that surrounds the Earth plane.

Our ancestors name some of these spheres as wrath, pride, envy, gluttony, greed, lust, and sloth or laziness, as shown in Figure 18. You can imagine all the pain and suffering that has been attributed to these different types of traumas. We are born into the Earth spheres, societal spheres, and cultural and religious spheres, as well as our generational family field. Once you incarnate through these relational fields around the Earth and incarnate into your family, the lower chakras activate your sense of trust, love, and acceptance and formulate all your beliefs and ideas about yourself.

The higher spheres of consciousness act as a template for the lower levels of your field. All of these fields or spheres of consciousness interact with each other and the core of your being through the seals of the chakras (chakra vortexes) and the emanating fields in your environment. You register trauma within the astral relational field as a natural response to the type of traumatic event.

The human experience can block love. From here, we form ideas and thoughts about the other that get stored in our belief systems, or we form ideas about ourselves: *I am unlovable; I am not enough; I am ugly.* This blocks the energy from coming into self-love from the core. Everything comes from the core to the holographic representation. I know oftentimes we think we're meditating up and out, but that is simply not true. It is the core star within us that is sending more light down to our natural experience, making us feel closer to God. As I meditate, I am trying to become more light; I am trying to be born again. Being born again means removing all these obstacles so I can transmit more light into this world. To be honest, I don't think humanity has birthed itself fully.

Think about any time you were frightened about something, no matter how big or small. What happened with your breath? Did you stop your breath or contract and hold it? Simultaneously with this contraction of breath, some feelings get held, and an assumption or belief about the situation is also formed. If this situation becomes prolonged and your core essence pulls away, in the words of Barbara Brennan, it curls in on itself.

The memory, impacted by unresolved thoughts and feelings, becomes embedded within your biofield; over time, these prolonged contracted energies can lead to disease. The prolonged energies on the fourth level of your HECF can impact your relationship with yourself and others. This level also acts as the bridge between the lower and higher levels, and it impacts your body at the cellular level—which leads us to the field of epigenetics again. When trauma is transmitted via morphogenetic resonance and within the fluid surrounding the DNA, it can change the structure of the DNA. We will explore how it impacts the lower levels of the field in the sections below.

The parable of the sower from the Bible is a great example of this. There was a sower who cast seeds on four different types of land: some on good soil, some on soil with thorns and thistles, some on rocks, and others on open fields. The seeds were the same, but the environment in which the seeds fell changed how the plants grew and produced. In the same way, the environment in which our DNA is developed can determine a lot about who we become. Think of the thorns and thistles as trauma in the family system of morphogenetic frequency; you are born on that land with the thorns and thistles. In such a situation, it will be a journey for you to remember all the goodness and blessings that you have within you.

Your astral body is like the A-field or memory of your life. This field stores all the memories from transgenerational patterns and past lives, and from incarnation, childhood, and onward. Unresolved trauma can be stored here, regulating unconscious behaviors and emotional and psychological reactivity. This is also a level where traumatic experiences become embedded and entangled, calling our attention to unhealthy behaviors, feelings, thoughts, or relationships that need healing.

The Tibetan Book of the Dead talks about higher or lower "bardo states of consciousness," indicating that there are spheres of consciousness within the fourth level, the bridge between both worlds. It's twofold: I have my relationship with the astral world, which is the unseen world, and I have all my relationships with everybody. So do you. This is where divine love transmits and changes frequency, becoming the expression of human love. When human love becomes entangled, our misconceptions, assumptions, painful feelings, and disappointment become embedded. The core light begins to contract here, curling in on itself. This is the start of ideas like *My parents don't love me, My boyfriend hates me,* or *I hate my parents and I love my parents.* Our love becomes bonded in both a negative and a positive way. The memory of the painful relationship acts as a shield to protect us from ever feeling that type of rejection again. Underneath these beliefs lie ideas like *I don't deserve love,* or *If my mother can't love me, how can anyone else?*

We decide to love one person over another. In doing so, our love toward the people we have not chosen to love does not disappear; rather, we contract it, hold it back, and surround it with painful images. The fourth level is all about the history of the relationships we had in our past, so we recreate those relationships from our childhood with people in our workplace and all around us. You can already see how that might start to lead to issues in any group situation. Each person walks into a room with a family and collective mind field that interacts with those of everyone else. You re-enact and create relationships based on your positive and negative past experiences. Everyone else is doing the same alongside you. We will explore how the trauma affects you in different situations in a future chapter so you can be aware and not allow it to impact how you are in life.

To identify entangled relationships that need healing, we will be using the I AM meditation and mantras. I will go over these in the next chapter, but they are important tools we can use to heal the trauma to which we have given space in our systems.

Trauma on the Third (Mental) Level

The third level is structured and is a replica of the seventh level, the divine mind. Human consciousness is encoded holographically throughout the third level of the human biofield. The seven chakra seals on the third level transmit and connect with our seventh level and our environment. This level encodes everything we have learned, consciously and unconsciously, in this lifetime, and connects with our family field and collective field to store all our experiences and knowledge.

Everything we've learned throughout every developmental stage—

in utero, birth, infancy, childhood, and adulthood—comes here: every book we've read, every TV show we've watched, and all the things that we've learned through religion and other affiliations. The third level also encodes all of our positive and negative beliefs, values, assumptions, and biases.

We are imprinted with all the historical wisdom and knowledge gathered at this level. In addition, we have access to wisdom that inspires us from the seventh level and the infinite intelligent universe. The knowledge we have then creates belief systems in our minds that shape how we see and frame the world. Robert Monroe, founder of the Monroe Institute, referred to these as "belief system territories," while Brennan referred to them as "fields of consciousness." All knowledge and all life has a mind field, including the moss under a tree and a unicellular amoeba.

Have you ever had any of the following thoughts? *I'm unlovable. I should not exist. I am unworthy. I am ugly. I am dumb. I don't have what it takes. I am always looked over at work. The world is scary.* All of them are entangled at this level and block you from progressing toward your goals. Our faulty belief systems and our misconceptions contribute to the time capsules that begin to appear as entangled or torn lines of light on the third level. These experiences remain contracted, freezing the traumatic experiences, feelings, and thoughts by storing them in the human biofield.

These unresolved experiences block our flow of creativity, love, and wisdom. When the seal of the third chakra is blocked, it can impact our sense of self-esteem, agency, and autonomy. We lose our direct divine connection and respect for the light within us. We start to seek approval outside ourselves and perform for others. Developmentally, we may become merged with others, or codependent, and repeat these learned patterns with those around us. Identifying our unhealthy beliefs about ourselves and others is key to unlocking the flow of wisdom and truth through the seals, awakening the divine quality of respect to open the seals on the third level. The third level also expresses all of our positive thoughts, values, and educational experiences.

As stated above, trauma can influence this layer by creating negative thought patterns and limiting beliefs, and by hindering the formation of positive beliefs that impact our feelings about ourselves. The flow of divine wisdom from the seventh level can be blocked until these lower-level entangled patterns are resolved. By accessing the seventh level, divine wisdom can help unblock the misconceptions and help realign you to higher truth and wisdom.

To adapt to trauma, we develop coping strategies and defenses that are based upon a fight, flight, freeze, fawn, or flop response. These responses are directly related to our creative life pulse, or how our energy naturally follows an expansion, stasis, contraction, stasis wave that correlates with our breath. When we experience trauma, our body's energy field contracts, then moves into survival mode. Our hara line then also shifts into a protective position as we contract. We have a natural protective mechanism that responds to any perceived threat from the outside. The mechanism is activated by the autonomic nervous system and prolongs contraction due to repeated patterns or trauma. The solution to fear is to defend by fleeing, fighting, freezing, fawning (caring for the abuser or others), or flopping (shutting down, collapsing, or fainting). This is why unhealed trauma can be detrimental to our health and well-being.

Consider any event that caused you distress, and reflect on how your breathing changed in that moment. You would have breathed shallowly with your upper chest, breathed rapidly, held your breath, or stopped breathing for prolonged periods. This action redirects your HECF into a protective stance, which is a natural solution to a perceived threat. Our core essence contracts then reforms in this defensive maneuver as a solution to the perceived threat. We need to consider that we are one energy, emerging from the core and appearing in several dimensions, fields, and matrices. Our core is our creative act; it contracts and builds defenses to protect us. These defenses are self-created, and they can be uncreated so the energy can be released into natural flow.

As previously stated, in *Core Light Healing*, Brennan describes this process whereby your core energy folds in on itself, creating a frozen time capsule of energy that is motivated by fear and encapsulates both the belief and your emotional reaction to that belief (Brennan, 2017). Paying attention to your breath can guide you toward these contacted and frozen energies to free the energy and your core qualities.

Relational trauma can impact the fourth, third, and second levels of our field, which store the memories and experiences about others and ourselves. On the second level, we will explore the feelings about self to recognize how love can become blocked or hidden beneath these contracted states.

Trauma on the Second (Emotional) Level

The emotional body is where the restoration of our feelings toward ourselves are stored and humble self-love and self-acceptance emanate. Early childhood and developmental trauma can create entangled feelings about ourselves. Humiliation, shame, self-hatred, self-judgment, and self-rejection can form dark clouds of energy in this level, blocking the energy flow from any of the chakras. Humiliation and shame can form around our sense of self, blocking the flow of self-love and self-respect. Any type of physical, emotional, sexual, or psychological abuse can cause dark clouds of energy to form within the field. This energy can holographically impact the whole field.

Developmentally, trauma at any stage can impact how we feel about ourselves. When love emerges from the seals of all seven chakras, the frequency of love, joy, and self-acceptance is essential for self-esteem and trust to flow. Physical, emotional, psychological, and relational abuse, loss, or trauma of any kind impacts how the flow of learning self-love and self-acceptance is developed throughout our life cycles.

Children learn love and acceptance from their parents, caregivers, friends, teachers, and mentors. The innate love flowing from the child's core through the seals of the chakras is met by love and acceptance from the people around them. When this is disrupted via any real or imagined rejection or abuse, the unresolved feelings and experiences coagulate and confuse the child, impacting their sense of self-worth, self-love, and self-acceptance.

The core qualities and transmission of divine love and relational love become suppressed within the child, which impacts the full cycle of love emerging from the core, transmitting into the sixth level, subscending into the fourth level, and meeting the incoming soul at the second level. It is here that love will return and touch the core of the child in a full cycle of infinite expression; this is what is meant by "core-to-core contact." The incoming baby and child came as a blessing, and their incoming light was not met in a full, infinite cycle. The child adapts by creating solutions, and their love becomes bonded in a negative way. This is how children learn to navigate becoming human; they can only love and bring blessings of light.

When the chakras on the second level are blocked, they will indicate the type of trauma and adaptation the child used to cope. The I AM mantra that opens the seals for self-love and self-acceptance can help recalibrate the flow of energy and love from the seals of the chakras, letting the light flow through the entire system again. This process can change and heal the entangled unresolved emotions and free you from years of self-judgment, shame, and blame. We will explore this further in the next chapter.

Trauma on the First (Physical) Level

The etheric body is the first layer and is where the physical body is formed. Trauma impacts the deep limbic system, brain, and nervous system. It appears as frayed or broken energy lines on the first level of the field, which can relate to different types of physical and psychological disease profiles.

Did you know that trauma changes who you are? Some of our brain's neurological connections are severed and new ones are formed when we go through trauma. The neuroplasticity of the brain tries to adapt and create new pathways to accommodate traumatic events as well as healthy ones. The changes will start with the mind but quickly trickle to affect your physical form and your general health. Remember, your genes are instructed on how to act by your chakra system.

On this first level of the field, we have trauma from things like car accidents, injuries, broken bones, and combat injuries. These have a direct impact on our physical body and the other fields as well. Physical trauma and injuries impact how we feel about ourselves, how we think, and how we relate to others. They can also impact our spiritual journey with doubt and fear. The whole vertical power current and chakra system is also disrupted when our bodies are in physical pain. The lines of energy that correlate to the fifth level are misaligned, especially with any damage to the physical body. This is where energy healing work can help repair and reduce healing time.

The first chakra directly relates to feeling safe in the world and our ability to trust. Trust moves from the root chakra up the vertical power current through the seals of each of the chakras. It is the base note of our incarnation and existence here on Earth. Any type of trauma can impact anyone's ability to trust. The seal of the first level on any chakra can close. Mistrust in the heart can block a person's ability to love again or forgive themselves. On the second level, if someone has experienced sexual abuse, it can be challenging for the person to trust or feel safe with a partner, and feelings of shame could arise.

On a neurological level, the autonomic nervous system goes into high gear, automatically shutting down the seals of the chakras while the hara shifts and the person moves into a survival maneuver. Each chakra on the first level adapts accordingly, depending on the person's life experiences; the divine quality of trust slows down, and the polarity of mistrust predominates. Here, it is important to understand how the I AM mantras are designed to awaken the suppressed quality within the divine genogram and family field around trust and safety.

Trauma impacts the structure and function of the brain, particularly the amygdala, hippocampus, and prefrontal cortex. Studies have shown that trauma can result in alterations in these brain regions, affecting emotional regulation, memory processing, and decision-making (Lowenstein et al., 1992). Think of times when people trauma block so they forget portions of their past, or when people with PTSD cannot stop thinking about situations they have been through. This is like when a computer disk is damaged and can no longer show the information in certain sections or keeps going back to the same section.

In addition, trauma disrupts the balance of neurotransmitters such as serotonin, dopamine, and norepinephrine in the brain. These chemical imbalances contribute to symptoms of anxiety, depression, and other mental health issues following trauma, which in turn contribute to the activation of the body's stress response system, leading to dysregulation of the HPA axis and abnormal cortisol levels. Prolonged exposure to stress hormones like cortisol can seriously impact immune function, metabolism, and mood regulation in the long term.

This leads us back to epigenetics. Trauma can result in epigenetic modifications, altering gene expression without changing the underlying DNA sequence. These changes influence your susceptibility to mental health disorders and other conditions related to trauma. In other words, your body starts to activate the codes that lead to disease and mental issues. But as Brennan stated: "The body is a self-healing organism, so it's really about clearing things out of the way so the body can heal itself" (*Brennan Healing Sessions*, n.d., para 1). If we find a way to align ourselves along the four dimensions, we can let the core light flow through and restore our health. Sometimes, the best thing we can do is allow ourselves to move past the trauma and reconnect through the hara to the core light again.

Before Brennan, in the early 1920s, Dr. Wilhelm Reich observed trauma in his friends who had faught in WWI, recognizing that their life force had become frozen. He was also a protégé of Freud, who had several theories, one of which concerned the libido. Reich's research saw the libido, our life force, and the human organism as essential to health and well-being. He saw that civilization and war caused people to reorient and suppress this force of energy, which he later renamed "orgone energy." He also explored how trauma and habitual adaptation created body armoring, where the breath and energy froze in the body. In chapter seven of my book *Cosmic Breath,* I speak about breath and the different contracted states. Here I go indepth on how to release these contracted states and how they show up in the five character/personality types.

Reich was the first to introduce the five character types, which Alexander Lowen and John Pierrakos later evolved to expand on the five character types.

Dr. Brennan trained extensively with both Lowen and Pierrakos, and committed her scientific mind to analyzing the four dimensions of humankind. She was a pioneer in the field, introducing the idea of the core star—core light emerging from the black velvet void of infinite intelligence.

The idea that trauma needs to be healed within the body is often associated with the field of somatic psychology. Various therapists and researchers, such as Peter Levine and Bessel van der Kolk, have contributed to this concept (van der Kolk, 2014). They emphasize the interconnection between the body and mind in processing and healing from trauma. Before this, trauma was believed to only affect the mind. People believed you could not get sick from what was in your mind, so healing from trauma was about working on your mind and nothing more. Kolk then showed that there was a connection between what happened in the mind and the body.

This opened up opportunities for more effective holistic healing when it comes to trauma. Trauma can lead to thoughts such as *I don't trust my parent anymore; they hurt me* or *I don't trust my boyfriend anymore*; I was hurt. But love doesn't go anywhere—it only gets suppressed by the trauma. Think of it this way: No medication can heal trauma at levels other than the physical. Pills cannot heal; they usually simply mask the symptoms until the root causes are addressed. These health challenges require the integration of new scientific approaches that provide data proving that working at the level of these invisible fields provides valuable results. The Heart Math Institute, a nonprofit organization, is currently providing revolutionary and sound scientific research on personal, social, and global coherency.

In the next chapter, let's explore how the divine qualities and I AM mantras are designed to bring coherency to your human biofield, impacting both your nervous system and your circulatory system.

Divine Qualities

Wisdom

Vision

Communication

Relational Love

Respect

Love and acceptance

Trust

Chapter 9:

Unveiling Divine Qualities

The light shone in the darkness, and the darkness has understood it not. –John the Apostle (John 1:5)

Visualize a dark room with no light coming in at all. Pitch black. Now imagine a flicker of light from a match being ignited and then brought to a torch. The light then keeps getting brighter and brighter until it completely fills the whole room. That is what is going to happen in your life as you allow your core to shine through and bring light into your physical body.

Yes, it is a transcendent experience. You will not be the same once the light emanates through you. The best part is that darkness— all the negative bonds, trauma, and hardships you have been through—cannot stop the light when it starts to shine through. In the same way that darkness leaves the room as soon as light is cast, so too will the darkness leave you. The light that comes from your core shines in beams of color that bring with them divine qualities, which will then be shared with the rest of the world. Think of yourself like a prism—a receiver of the pure light from within who is then able to express that light in the form of the divine qualities in your life.

In this chapter, we will look at the seven essential divine qualities crucial for healing and restoration in individuals. These are what will replace the trauma that we covered in the last chapter. We need to not just remove the trauma from our lives but also replace it with the light that comes from the core, through the human biosystem, to manifest in our lives.

Figure 19: The I AM Mantras

Practice the I AM Meditation for Healing

Most trauma comes from our childhood, and it is then embedded within the chakra system and human energy consciousness field (HECF). The chakras store these patterns of trauma deep within the field and are also impacted by the family and collective fields. Releasing these traumas requires the transformational work of self-discovery and the transcendental work of illumination. Just as transfiguration occurs the moment your core light enters into the incarnation process, engaging each of the four dimensional stages from light and energy consciousness into the physical realm, memories are imprinted into each of the dimensions. Your core light navigates this metamorphosis, becomes entangled in these contracted and unhealed memories, and adapts by creating solutions, like defenses, that reorganize around the traumatic event and register it as dangerous.

These records are stored within the physical body and the human energy consciousness system (HECS). As a result, the innate divine qualities are redirected into negative love patterns etched upon our autonomic and somatic nervous systems, which record, respond, or react to environmental stressors. The child's field becomes entangled with the family, transgenerational, and collective fields. Transfiguration happens when we unravel these entangled patterns and restore the divine qualities within.

In order to understand this phenomenon better, let us look at it from a biological perspective. The brain has a map that can help us understand how trauma gets stored in our systems, but also how we can release it. The I AM meditations channel the energy of the practice to have a biological and neurological effect on your brain and physiological being.

Let's take a bird's eye view of our brain and nervous system to help us anchor our meditation practices toward self-mastery of the I AM meditations and chants, and to move us into the "middle way" or what many wisdom teachers identify as "nondualism." The theories that support the I AM meditations revisit the ancient wisdom sages.

After 35 years of teaching and working with private clients, I noticed that many students and clients had difficulty changing certain patterns. Fortunately, I found Dr. Amen's book, *Change Your Brain Change Your Life* (Amen, 2016), which inspired me to reconceptualize the way I approached working with students and clients. These behaviors, which you may also have challenges getting over, are called automatic negative thoughts, and they have a strong impact on the HECF. Likewise, trauma has a physiological and psychological impact on the brain. As we have discussed, modern research shows concrete links between our ancestors, our emotions, and our very being. In fact, Amen refers to the brain as "the hardware to our soul; when the brain is compromised with automatic negative thoughts (ANTs), the soul cannot truly be expressed." I agree that our divine potential is processed within our brains and transmitted to all our other senses and bodily systems. In one lecture, Amen says (and I paraphrase his words) that it is not that the person's soul doesn't want to express its divine beauty; it is that the malfunctions in the brain don't allow it. He suggests several types of treatment for changing negative brain patterns, from medication to meditation and prayer.

Another physician and author, Charles L. Whitfield, MD, postulates in his book *The Truth About Mental Illness* that childhood abuse and prolonged trauma and stress contribute to most mental health issues today (Whitfield, 2004). Generational trauma not only impacts us genetically but is also mapped within the HECF. Our brains adapt to these situations and look for ways to adapt and survive. We are born to thrive, yet our survival instinct activates whenever there is a perceived threat to our survival.

Before the emergence of epigenetics, where genetic researchers study the changes that occur on top of the genetic code, Dr. Bruce Lipton's book *Biology of Belief: Unleashing the Power of Consciousness, Matter, and Miracles*—which we have learned from in the previous chapters—theorized how our memories, thoughts, and emotions related to a traumatic event can travel across the fluid membrane that surrounds our DNA (Lipton, 2005). Lipton suggests that the fluid around our cells carries other awareness, beyond the genetic code, that is correlated to our health.

Today, the study of epigenetics and neuropsychology is at the forefront of science and consciousness studies, and it includes how our transgenerational patterns of traumatic events impact our genetic transmission. As early as the 1990s, Dr. Candace Pert described in her book *Molecules of Emotion: The Science Behind Mind–Body Medicine* how our brain becomes habituated or addicted to the chemicals produced by certain emotions (Pert, 2003). The brain acts as if it is hungry to recreate certain situations to maintain a specific balance, feeding off those emotions. You can see how fragile our brains are when exposed to long periods of stress. Our natural divine nature, the matrix of life, is mapped with these experiences and hidden beneath a sea of this type of unhealthy programming, as explored in *Blessings From a Thousand Generations*.

Research by philosopher Eva Jablonka and biologist Marion Lamb (1999), as presented in their book *Epigenetic Inheritance and Evolution: The Lamarckian Dimension*, suggests that genes are far more fluid and responsive to the environment than we have realized. Information can be transmitted to descendants in other ways than the base sequence of DNA; interactions are stored in the cellular membrane of a newborn baby. I used this illustration in *Blessings From a Thousand Generations*, referring to when an infant is bumped and cries, feels, and expresses pain. Unconsciously, the mother responds quickly, scoops up the baby, and soothes them by rocking. Within the subconscious mapping, the baby associates soft touch, words, and love with less pain. On the other hand, when the mother misreads the cues and tries to soothe the baby by feeding them, the limbic system can correlate food with less pain, which sets up a negative pairing or bond of needing food to reduce pain. Repetitions of these need–response interactions become literally embedded, or wired, within our cellular memory.

All of these studies paved the way for us to understand not only how trauma is stored in our systems, but also how we can unblock the flow and bring the divine qualities to the light. This is the commandment of Jesus: to allow our light to radiate through and change our lives and those of the people around us. So, let's take a look at the brain and understand a few fundamental features that are important for self-mastery, transforming habitual patterns, and recalibrating your HECF toward your divine nature, the infinite intelligent field, the field of transfigurative love, and your divine design.

The Brain Structure & Trauma

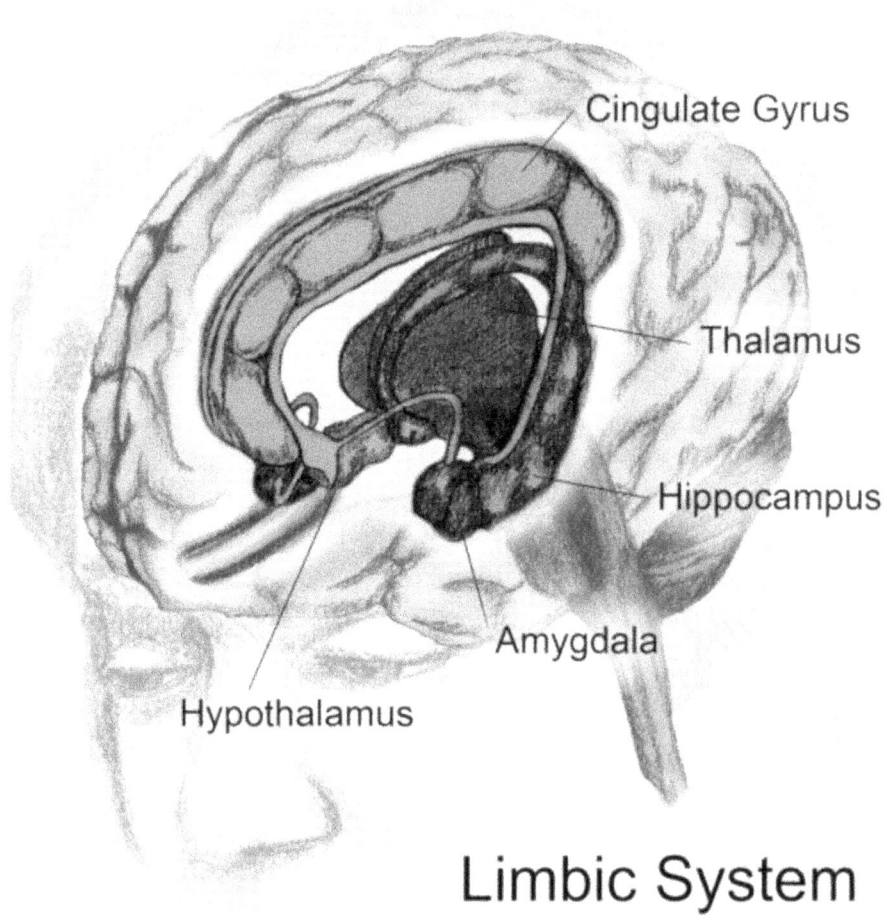

Figure 20: Human Brain

Our most basic emotions, memories, and instincts develop within the brain in the limbic system. Our innate behaviors—which accommodate bonding, nourishment, processing responses to thoughts and emotions, survival versus thriving responses, and fight, flight, freeze, or fawn responses—are mapped within this system, which coordinates the behavioral, autonomic (involuntary), and hormonal adjustments required to maintain homeostasis or normal operation. When we experience the basic emotions of love, pleasure, hunger, or fear, the limbic system releases neurohormones throughout the body and changes occur in the respiratory system, circulatory system, nervous system, and immune system. For example, when children smell their mother (through the olfactory nerve and the limbic system), they respond with both cardiorespiratory and gastrointestinal-related activity. In other words, their emotional and visceral nervous systems are directly impacted by the interactive sensory world they share with their mother.

Our brains record this bonding in the deep limbic system. Using the chemicals of love and bonding for survival, a recycled negative event is recorded in the brain as love based on fear, replacing a more positive bond of love based on nurturance, security, and trust. Unraveling the mystery of our familial and ancestral heritage allows us to recover our spiritual heritage and frees us from bondage to the negative patterns transmitted generationally. Even our responses and concept of God or spirituality can be mapped within the brain. The neuroplasticity of our brains has the innate capacity to learn and heal.

In their groundbreaking book *How God Changes Your Brain: Breakthrough Findings from a Leading Neuroscientist*, Andrew Newberg, MD, and Mark Robert Waldman (2010) researched six different structures of the brain to understand whether the concepts of God and spirituality impact the brain. Their research included scanning the brains of several participants; they found that those who believed in God, those who meditated and prayed, and even atheists would activate the same parts of the brain when visualizing God. It was discovered that our frontal lobe, limbic system, anterior cingulate gyrus, amygdala, thalamus, and parietal lobe are impacted by our thoughts of God or spirituality. Newberg and Waldman suggest that the more we meditate and pray, the more likely we are to experience a mystical or transcendental state, and that these states can be measured by taking SPECT brain scans during these peak experiences.

I imagine our brains respond holographically to our divine nature and bond in positive and healthy ways. By meditating on and chanting the I AM mantras, we can influence and change our habitual unhealthy patterns. When we do so, we release our negative thoughts, feelings, and behaviors as well as the entangled transgenerational negative love bonds. This process frees our deep limbic system to express the divine design of our life. We are restored and move beyond trauma, reclaiming our innate birthright of infinite intelligence, transfigurative love, and the divine design of our life. Our brain is wired for divine and spiritual experiences and expression. When these three aspects flow from our essence, we create positive love bonds; when our human energy and consciousness becomes entangled with unhealthy habitual patterns, thoughts, and emotions, our love bonds to those negative events. Let's take a deeper dive into exploring negative love bonds.

As we outlined in the previous chapters, we are cosmic beings, seedpods of divinity, incarnating as human beings. When we reclaim our birthright, the cosmos, we open the windows of light within our chakra system to fully incarnate as light beings. As humans, our light has not fully incarnated; rather, it becomes blocked, suppressed, or misdirected due to the negative love bonds and quantum entanglements that occurred as we courageously navigated becoming human.

Negative love bonds are any unhealthy habitual behaviors, thoughts, or emotions that inhibit our life force from flowing naturally. They arise from our misconceptions about life in early childhood, or from adult trauma or abuse, and are rooted in love, deep limbic bonding, and our interpersonal need for others. They are based on unresolved conflicts, behaviors, feelings, and beliefs that became the norm of our earliest childhood memories and teen or adult experiences, and which dictate how we perceive ourselves and others. Our cones of perception or biases are shaped by previous personal or interpersonal experiences. Our innate ability to love unconditionally becomes bonded with these misconceptions, emotions, and attachment behaviors.

The seedpod of divinity encompasses all the divine qualities within the universal life force. Our whole existence flows from the infinite intelligent field of consciousness, transfigurative love, and the divine design of the universe. We are going to look at how you can use the I AM mantras to open the sacredness of who you are by releasing the negative love bonds that hold you hostage to thoughts, beliefs, emotions, behaviors, and relationships that inhibit the flow of divine consciousness from you.

In Figure 20, earlier in this section, you will notice the cingulate gyrus, which looks like a peapod and acts like a railway station—it picks up thoughts and emotions, then activates the navigational system that sends signals to systems in the body. Habitual thoughts and emotions get bottlenecked, going back and forth without the cingulate gyrus switching the station the information needs to be sent to. In response, the amygdala becomes overactivated with certain emotions in a repetitive pattern. Everyone is plagued with ruminating now and then, but for some this habitual habit of automatic negative thinking becomes compulsive and crippling. In meditating on and chanting the I AM mantras, we do not deny these habitual patterns; rather, we observe them and their impact on our senses and bodily systems.

Once we identify the pattern, we are ready to start the chanting and meditation practice. We will repeat the chant several times, allowing for the opposite thought to rise and fall without judgment. You see, it's like a skip in your favorite album: You've played that song so many times that another groove has formed, and the needle cannot move beyond it to play the full song. When this happened, I remember being frustrated and going to pick up the needle to move it one ridge so the rest of the album would play—or, because I loved the song so much, I would play it again.

Your cingulate gyrus works in the same way. You may need to repeat the mantra several times, moving back and forth from your unhealthy habitual thought to the healthy thought or mantra. This helps you reprogram your system, enabling your brain and deep limbic system to begin to create the pathway that will lead to a breakthrough. You demagnetize the habitual pattern and open the pathway for your innate divine qualities to restore the divine design of your brain and different systems of the body. The divine design of your HECS is restored, just like restoring the hard drive on a computer.

Review the diagrams of the brain, body, nervous system, and the human chakra and energy system, as they will be helpful while visualizing and directing your breath. The vibrational frequencies of the mantras are transmitted up the central channel of your body, moving from the base of your spine all the way up your nervous system and into your deep limbic system.

In my practice, I notice that insight and transcendence often bring temporary relief to my clients. To transfigure these patterns, the healing work needs to go much deeper and release the physical patterns stored in the brain and nervous system. By repeating the I AM mantras to access the chakra energy system and identify faulty feelings and beliefs, the negative love bond patterns are released and the core light is restored.

In the next section, we will go over each of the divine qualities, including the mantra that you can use during your meditations to open that chakra on all levels. For now, let us talk about how you use those mantras in the meditation process. As we do this, we will be breathing in the divine quality. For example, you will start with breathing in trust from your roots, then breathe it up into the brain and the deep limbic system.

You can try it now. Instead of the breaths you take normally, try to take a deep breath and bring it to your brain. The deep limbic system, the basal ganglia, and the cingulate gyrus will activate the counter quality to what you are breathing in. That is, if you breathe in trust, you may find that there is mistrust in your mind. As you say, "I AM trust" and breathe in, your mind will respond by showing that you do not trust anyone.

You can realize where there is a block in your life by shining a light to see your thoughts. You should never hide things in the fog. When we do not think about where we do not trust, we might not even know that there are areas where we are distrusting. When you say, "I AM trust," you are testing to see if that statement aligns with what is in your mind. If you are not trusting in one area or another, it will be highlighted as you recite the mantra. You might realize that you don't trust your partner, employees, boss, or family. Only then will you realize that past experiences have wired you to look at everything as untrustworthy.

Let's now explore your innate power to heal. As you start to identify that you mistrust, don't deny it; instead, let it come out. Acknowledge that you have areas where you do not trust, and let that acknowledgement out. Say it out loud, even: "I do not trust anyone." And then, after that comes out a little bit, you can breathe back in the trust in the I AM that I AM.

If you repeat the process three or more times, your brain will start to recalibrate. You will get to where the polarity becomes neutralized in the center of the fulcrum. The imbalance between trust and mistrust synchronizes into balance. This would be the same with the other divine qualities as well. Sometimes I love and accept myself and others, but sometimes I don't. You have to bring both extremes to the fulcrum and the center.

The question is, how do you come to the fulcrum of the center rather than being at one of the two ends of the polarity? In the meditation, you use your breath and the mantra to see which negative beliefs are in your mind already. In life, we repeat things over and over and ruminate until those ideas are a part of who we are. This meditation practice will help you reverse that process and flush out any beliefs that should not be in your mind, allowing you to clear out the negativity that comes up when you breathe in the mantra.

The brain is very important; it is like the computer carrying all the programs for your life. When you tap into your mind, it gives you the program and you can then implement it. There are things we learned in childhood and have reaffirmed throughout our lives. Imagine an idea playing in your mind for years and getting etched into your brain. You have to recognize that this programming is in your mind so you can deal with it. Most people don't bring the new quality into their brain to free and unlock it because they do not even realize they have the divine quality curled in. We can change this by rebalancing the polarity—and, eventually, that program will stop running in our minds.

I have used these mantras for myself, and I have seen great change and freedom through them. I used to ruminate a lot, but now not as much. As I used the I AM mantras to unblock my chakras on all levels, I brought the extremes to the center, balancing out the polarities. I've reprogrammed my mind, and you can do so too. You have to understand your imperfections and love both yourself and your imperfections to come back to perfection. You have to actively want to activate these core qualities. I have resources on my website (donnaevansstrauss.com) that can take you through how to use the I AM mantras and meditations step by step until you bring your core divine qualities to flow in your life.

Let's now explore the seven divine qualities and corresponding I AM mantras designed to release the negative love bonds and restore the light within. We'll then discuss the power of forgiveness as a way to free your core qualities and have them shine through. We can use specific mantras and meditation practices to free us from unhealthy habitual patterns. The integration of these ideas, which are also explored in *Blessings From a Thousand Generations*, creates a consciousness field that is an unending resource of prayers, loving-kindness, compassion, mercy, and grace that is available to all sentient life and can awaken within us. In my search for truth and self-mastery, the mantras that I share in the following section came to me during meditation.

The Seven Innate Divine Qualities

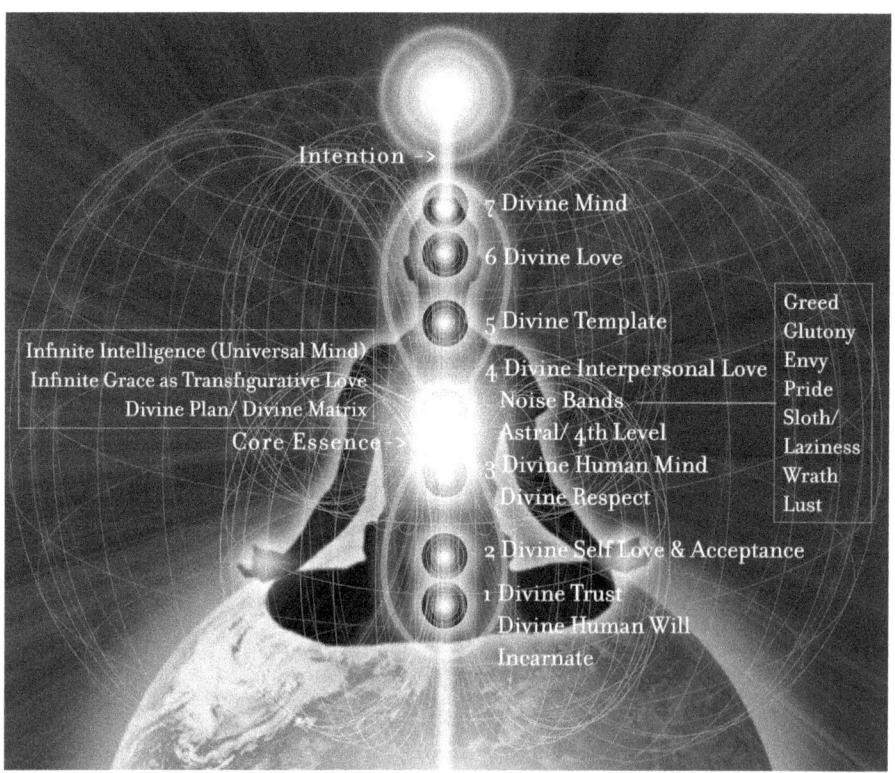

Figure 21: Seven Divine Qualities

You now understand that there can be blockages in your system at different levels, which affect you in distinctive ways, but what is it that is being blocked from shining through? You know at your core there are all these divine and powerful qualities that help you to shine in everything you do, but what are they?

In this section, we will describe each of the seven divine qualities: divine trust, divine self-love and self-acceptance, divine respect, divine relational love, divine communication, divine vision, and divine wisdom. We will look at where they come from and why they are important to your healing. We will also explore how they open the seven seals of the chakras on all seven levels, releasing the divine qualities that have been suppressed by trauma. We will also study how to use the I AM mantras to unfold these qualities and become an instrument of divine grace and peace. You can review Figure 21 to locate the chakra that we are discussing in conjunction with each quality.

Now that you know what the divine qualities are, and before we explore each one in depth, let me explain how they work together and open the seals of your chakras. I rename these seals "windows of light," since it is here that the direct transmission from the Divine emerges into the earthly plane. These chakras, or "flowers of life," are informational transporting systems communicating from the core star realm of existence into the Earth plane. It's quite simple when you think about it; the information has always been there for us to discover. Each divine quality opens the seven seals of all the chakras on the level of that quality.

Divine trust is essential to opening all seven windows of light on the first level of the field. Trust is essential for all chakras to open, and it is key to understanding when a particular chakra is blocked from the natural flow of energy moving from the core dimension, and also in the receptive flow from the environment. The same is true with all of the seven divine qualities and their impact on each level of the human energy field. Remember, each chakra and level correlates to a physical, emotional, psychological, relational, and spiritual function.

During traumatic experiences, these chakras and the field become occluded with unresolved or undigested memories and feelings, which become embedded in the field. The divine qualities and

I AM mantras help us identify these frozen experiences, and we learn to move through the transformation, transcendence, and transfiguration process. This process will require your commitment and focus; it takes time, space, patience, and a willingness to uncover the light within you.

Once you discover this method and work with these mantras, you will find pleasure in how simple the process becomes. You may need to explore several uncomfortable thoughts, feelings, and memories at first, but if you stay committed to working through the polarities held within your painful experiences, you will free yourself from the negative love bonds and release your divine potential. Let's get started.

Divine Trust

The first chakra and first level of the field is a mirror image of the fifth chakra and fifth level. As stated in the previous chapter, it is here that we learn to align our free will with the divine will. Trust emerges deeply from the core of our being and is a foundational quality for health and well-being. As the saying goes, "Trust me; I am closer than the breath in your nostrils." If we surrender to divine trust, we allow this quality to emerge from deep within our core. We are not dependent on our own doing but rather on God, who resides within the foundation of our being.

Trust, like the rest of the divine qualities, comes through the windows of light of the chakras. The seals of the chakras have access to each level of the field. The center of the seal of the chakra has a Flower of Life opening from the core essence of the first level of the field. Each chakra on the first level, which is blue, allows the flow of divine trust coming from the core essence.

Consider for a moment that you do not make more trust in the world. You either trust or don't trust. You can play with this idea by exploring how in one moment you can trust one person, and in the next, you don't trust. Who is regulating trust and shutting down the flow of this divine quality? You have the power of free will and self-will. When you experienced trauma in life, your field contracted and you pulled down the shades over those windows of light. It was an instant choice as a solution to protect yourself. These innate responses are necessary for survival yet can become habitual responses. So, I always tell my clients, "You do not make more trust in the world; rather, you allow the frequency to flow from the depths of your core. Trust is an innate quality and your birthright."

Throughout our life cycle, we encounter situations where we learn to mistrust others or our environment. When this happens, the deep limbic system records these memories in our unconscious as mistrust, fear, or danger. The brain, which functions like a mainframe computer program, responds to subtle signals that activate a reactive response. We contract in this reactive response, activating the belief that a person or situation is dangerous. Many times, this reactivity is an old program based on an earlier developmental experience.

Our signal anxiety and over-reactivity give us a clue to the mistrust that is wired in our brain, nervous system, and HECF. Depending on how the trust is affected, it will contract in distinct ways on different levels. Factors like how we are raised and taken care of or the conditions we grow up in will determine how the trust develops. If you grow up in lack, you might then fail to trust that you will ever have enough, which creates the contracting described above. Trust starts to get suppressed, and the nervous system starts to wire in and develop mistrust. This process can be unconscious, and can happen at any stage of your life.

The I AM Mantra for Divine Trust

The I AM mantra for trust is "I AM divine trust and I trust in the I AM that I AM." As you meditate, you will be able to bring the two extreme ends of the spectrum to the center. Where you used to think you could not trust anyone ever, you will start to change that programming and learn that you can trust some people sometimes. This does not mean you are going to be naive and trust everyone all the time. No—you will need to accept both ends of the polarity, so you are not completely trusting but also not completely distrusting.

Divine Self-Love & Self-Acceptance

The second chakra opens when divine love subscends into human love and is then experienced as self-love and self-acceptance. Divine self-love and self-acceptance develop from birth throughout early childhood. This is the foundation of Christ's second commandment, "Love thy neighbor as thyself." You cannot love your neighbor until you have learned to love yourself.

Transfigurative love and grace are our birthright and emerge from our core as a blessing. You are a blessing! This love subscends through you into the Earth plane from the sixth level, to the fourth level, and into the second level. As we discussed in the previous chapters, so much can transpire during the incarnation and developmental stages. Because of this, recovering our innate gift of love requires a commitment to working with our genogram—identifying the negative love bonds, exploring the divine qualities that were suppressed, and using the I AM mantra to restore your birthright. Experiencing humble self-love and self-acceptance brings you closer to union with your divine core; you actually experience communion with the light within you. The transformation and transcendence process is complete as you dissolve what separates you from God or the infinite intelligent universe that unites us all.

We usually develop self-love and self-acceptance or self-rejection. The idea, though, is to find the polarity of the two and how we bring that polarity back into the core of the chakra. Think about the shape of the infinity sign—it has two equal sides that meet in the center, and in the same way, we need to bring both of these extremes to the center of the chakra.

Let's explore how to heal the polarity between self-love and self-acceptance and self-hate or unworthiness through the mantra for divine self-love and self-acceptance below.

The I AM Mantra for Divine Self-Love & Self-Acceptance

The I AM mantras for this level are "I AM divine self-love and self-acceptance" and "I love and accept the I AM that I AM."

Divine Respect

The third chakra and level, or the human mind field, is an imprint of the seventh level awaiting human developmental experiences. It also reflects how we relate to others and feel our place in the world. When we respect and know the divine light within us, the window of light opens and allows a two-way flow of consciousness. Our authentic sense of autonomy and agency in the world requires us to remember that our true source of power and individuation arises from the core of our being. Divine respect is essential to clearing and opening the third chakra and third level. Here, the divine mind and the human mind are harmonized.

During the stages of our development, we lose our connection to the light within. This occurs in many ways as we navigate being human. We start adapting to our parents, relatives, teachers, friends at school, and so on. During these stages, our third level is scripted with all types of learned knowledge, from our value system to our religious affiliations, and the beliefs and biases of our family, our culture, and the society in which we live. During this process, we can lose the connection to our authentic selves. When we add trauma or adaptation patterns to this equation, we can feel further away from our core; our sense of self in the universe is configured around our environment rather than our core or the universe emerging from within.

This often shows up as codependent behavior toward everybody around us, such as waiting to see what others are doing first and following what they are doing. Our intuition and other gifts arise from the third chakra; when it becomes occluded, self-doubt occurs, and all the superego judgments block the creative flow of our intuitive wisdom from being transmitted when the seventh level, the divine mind, informs the third level of our human mind.

The third chakra is also where self-doubt comes in. This can inhibit your ability to make decisions. Instead of following the intuitive flow of information communicating to you from all your life experiences and your core, you look for approval from your environment. You seek outside confirmation and begin to close the window of light and information flowing from within. The correct orientation is "I trust the Divine to author my life" rather than "I trust the outside to tell me what to do or approve of me."

The I AM Mantra for Divine Respect

The I AM mantra for this divine quality is "I AM divine respect and I respect the I AM that I AM."

Divine Relational Love

The fourth chakra is the bridge between the higher cosmic realms and the lower earthly realms. As previously stated, the transmission of divine love subscends into the fourth level as human love. Divine–human love is expressed when you relate to others from the core of your being. All the different types of relationships are within the memory field of the fourth level. The fourth chakra is the bridge between Heaven and Earth. It is the portal from which we incarnate and bring love and blessings into this world.

When the first three divine qualities are blocked, divine relational love will not flow freely. Consider for a moment when a relationship was disappointing or you felt your heart was broken. Trust is usually the first window of light to close. You start to carry the pain of mistrust deep within the heart chakra, where the memory of the heart break is stored. Then, you bargain between not loving the other or blaming and not loving yourself. Thinking or feeling there is something wrong within you, you close the window of light of self-love and self-acceptance and then create a negative belief about yourself or the other, losing a deeper connection with divine respect.

This process becomes stored deeply in the heart chakra as an unhealed memory, and it then resides there, blocking the flow of love emerging from the core. If you have recurring patterns of heartbreak and loss, the chakra and field become murky until healing occurs. Each of the I AM mantras is designed to restore the divine quality and release the negative love bonds or polarity that shrouds the light and relational love flowing from you. By healing these different levels, you awaken and share your innate divine qualities and release the powerful flow of relational love. Your relationships open to a flow of pleasure and joy and you become less reactive to situations that once activated you. You have transfigured the past and are free to love in the present.

Simply remember that divine trust, self-love and self-acceptance, and respect open the windows of light on the first three levels of your human biofield. These are the foundational innate qualities that allow the flow of your true self. The coherence and clarity of these three levels are the basis of healthy relational love. When we are entangled in relational challenges, painful memories from childhood, and adult trauma, our divine qualities and sense of self become mired in unresolved physical, emotional, and psychological challenges. Now, you have an opportunity to change these patterns and reclaim the light within.

Remember, love is always flowing; our painful memories are only entangled in negative love bonds from the past. Your essential nature is infinite love and grace—infinite intelligence that unfolds the Flower of Life into the moment of the now. You are a fractal of the divine design of the universe coming as a blessing to the Earth. The trauma we talked about in the previous levels, and the associated unforgiveness, resentment, shame, and other negative love bonds, holds us back from experiencing divine qualities for ourselves and sharing them at the fourth level.

The I AM Mantra for Divine Relational Love

These powerful I AM mantras allow the window of light to open so the power of transfigurative love can flow through you. Let's explore a couple: "I relate to others from the I AM that I AM" and "I AM divine relational love." These mantras free you from any negative love bonds and open your heart to express blessings here on Earth.

Divine Communication

The fifth chakra transmits the divine matrix and divine will, and is directly related to divine communication. On a human level, it correlates to how we communicate from our divine core. We speak and hear truth from the Divine within us.

The fifth chakra is about being able to communicate correctly. Can

I speak my truth? Do I hear the truth or do I hear with judgment? Am I listening for what's wrong with the conversation? Am I listening only to jump up and tell somebody something rather than really listening from the core? Am I hearing beneath the words somebody's telling me? All these are questions you need to ask yourself as you go through the meditations for divine communication.

Here, we look at how we connect with the higher power and the purpose of our existence. The universe has plans for us, shared through a special framework that represents our humanity. This communication comes from a deeper level of awareness that humans typically don't understand. The universe shares knowledge with us in a way that goes beyond our basic understanding. Our potential as humans springs from this everlasting presence and creative energy. We come into existence from a creative thought. Scientific studies of the complex universe and the design of humanity help us in our growth as individuals and as a species.

These cosmic messages travel faster than light. You are made of light, a part of the Divine created to live as a human. By overcoming the limits of your lower energy levels, you naturally open up to the flow of divine light and wisdom from the higher realms.

Let's first explore how to improve communication in your energy field. These practices help clear the way for better communication in your relationships. How we connect with others and how we see ourselves lays the groundwork for receiving creative ideas from a universal source. When we struggle to listen and communicate meaningfully in our relationships, it can also make it harder to connect with the higher parts of our consciousness.

Take a moment to think about how you listen and how others interpret your words. Do you find it hard to feel heard? Do you hold back from speaking up, or maybe talk too much without considering others' views? Past experiences, especially painful ones, can affect our ability to express ourselves, impact our sense of identity, and influence our relationships and careers. When we bring past limitations into our present interactions, we block our connection to the higher realms.

The I AM Mantra for Divine Communication

The I AM mantra for this divine quality is "I communicate from the I AM that I AM; I AM divine communication. I speak and hear the truth from the I AM that I AM."

Divine Vision

The sixth chakra relates to divine vision and divine love and directly relates to the infinite grace upwelling from your core. It helps you open your eyes to see clearly from your divine center. Do you trust what you are seeing, or are you paranoid and looking for danger all the time?

Divine vision directly correlates to the infinite intelligence emerging from your core essence. It is a direct connection to universal consciousness and opens us to higher wisdom and knowledge that is unknown on the earthly plane. From here, new scientific discoveries and creative inventions emerge that solve world problems. Consider the evolution of consciousness over the past hundred years. We have moved from the invention of the first plane to landing on the moon, and from the invention of computer science to the internet, the World Wide Web, and AI. All of this new information is accessible when we expand into the higher realms of consciousness with our curiosity. The answers are already awaiting our discovery.

When you do not press in to receive this knowledge, however, you will feel stuck. It will be as if you cannot develop new ideas, solutions, or methods to push your career and objectives forward. You could get stuck thinking that you cannot do anything or that you are not smart enough to come up with new ideas. The way out of this is by releasing any blocks that stop the flow of energy through this chakra on all levels.

The I AM Mantra for Divine Vision

The I AM mantra for divine vision is "I AM divine vision; I see truth from the I AM that I AM."

Divine Wisdom

The seventh chakra relates to divine wisdom and is directly connected to universal consciousness and infinite intelligence. Trusting in the divine mind has to do with trusting in that download of divinity: "I am made in the image and likeness of God." So, our golden grid structure is a replica of the infinite intelligent universe.

Our higher consciousness imparts insights into our human awareness through intuitive understanding. Many of us encounter moments of clarity and realization that appear to emerge spontaneously—for example, anticipating a phone call just before it comes through, or thinking about a challenging situation until the solution suddenly reveals itself in a moment of inspiration. This can happen in the shower, during a walk, or as you fall asleep.

Some of the most common ways we block our divine wisdom is through trauma, which leads to disbelief in the infinite universe, failure to trust, selfishness, self-doubt, ego or arrogance, and overthinking. If your chakras are blocked on the lower levels, then direct wisdom will also be blocked.

The I AM Mantra for Divine Wisdom

The mantra for unblocking this chakra is "I AM divine wisdom; I know the truth from the I AM that I AM."

Example From CB

In chapter seven, when we created the divine genogram, we looked at an example of CB, who created her genogram and uncovered the areas where the blessings were blocked in her life. She was able to unravel the divine qualities in her life, and below I share how this revelation looks for her.

Divine Trust

CB encountered many challenges during the first stages of incarnation. Her parents decided to give her up for adoption, and later she discovered that her biological mother isolated herself from the family. Some members were unaware of the pregnancy and her birth. To this day, CB prefers the wooded sanctuary that surrounds her home rather than engaging with other people. In this way, she has a subconscious bond with her mother's field. Her adoptive parents offered her a home, yet she was often met with opposition growing up.

She tried expressing herself when her adoptive grandfather abused her but was met with disbelief. These early experiences left her unable to trust and feel safe. She often kept her disclosures to herself and began retreating inside. Who could she trust? In her work, CB learned how to unravel these embedded beliefs about safety and trust. By working with the mantras, she learned to change her brain chemistry and chose to access trust from her divine core. She began to feel her essence and welcome herself into this world, acknowledging her divine light and presence.

Divine Self-Love & Self-Acceptance

You can imagine how CB must have felt when she tried to talk about the abuse but was met with denial rather than safety and support. Her natural gift of loving became bonded with shame, unhealthy guilt, and darkness. Her natural impulse for love was shrouded over by her family field and she lost her innate connection to Divine love, human love, and self-love. By exploring and uncovering these painful memories, she found her way home, to her core, and innate ability to love and accept herself. To dissolve the learned disapproval and shame and restore her divine presence, CB cleared her biofield and reprogrammed her deep limbic system. She found a way to embrace these events and reclaim the light within.

Divine Respect

When CB was growing up she bonded her love with many faulty assumptions about herself. She began to doubt her true nature and instead of being mirrored by her family, she longed to find someone in the environment to respect and reflect her core. She had to conquer her low self-esteem by restoring divine respect, finding her deeper connection to her core qualities, and respecting the light from within. She identified, rescripted her faulty assumptions, and began working on empowering herself to change these patterns and change the cycles of unhealthy thoughts, ruminations, and faulty thinking. She could now live from her divine presence and had tools to use from moment to moment when confronted with uncomfortable situations. She was able to identify the difference between the events that happened and her self-definition.

Divine Relationships

CB's family mind field from both her biological and adoptive parents transmitted several sequences of relationship patterns forming around both positive and negative love bonds. Her earliest relationships were met with invasiveness and abuse. Through her early teen years, she encountered many unhealthy relationships. Yet, later she was able to overcome many of these challenges and marry a wonderful man with whom she is raising children. As she is embracing her healing work, she has faced some of the most difficult situations that have inhibited her from exploring and feeling safe around awakened intimacy. CB continues to explore relationships with others outside of her family and works towards securing healthy relationships and trust with women and men. CB has opened her heart with trust, self-love, self-acceptance, and respect as the base notes of feeling authentic in relationships. Restoring these qualities clears the way to live in the moment and clears the residue of mistrust in her relationships. She continues to enjoy her life living in a secluded area.

Divine Communication

CB has learned how to open her throat chakra to speak her truth. She can hold the frequencies of love, and respect while listening to others. She is able to navigate and take in authentic love from others and not close off when she feels hurt. She also understands that even when others may not believe her, she can believe in herself. She can create safe boundaries with others and not overreact in situations where she may feel rejected or unheard. She can speak from the clarity of light inside where all the divine qualities are flowing through her communications.

Divine Vision

When defended, CB could see the world as a dangerous place. She was sensitive to rejection and on alert for any type of abuse. By reorganizing her vision and the center of the chakra with the preceding divine qualities, CB was able to see the light within others. Now all rejection passes her by without having a visceral anxiety response and falling into a rabbit hole of unhealthy thoughts. Her eyes were open to see clearly and to see others with a clear lens. When trust, love, and respect are shrouded we don't see situations as clear. By restoring these qualities CB frees herself to see others from their divine presence through her divine presence. There is a reorientation of the deep limbic system and visual cortex to coherency and balance.

Divine Wisdom

When CB opens to divine wisdom to flow from the crown chakra and 7th level of her field, she is engaged at the highest level of her coherency. CB often felt disconnected here, until clearing the negative love bonds, reactivity, and earlier programming. Now it is open to universal wisdom to flow through her and guide her life. This wisdom balances her unhealthy thoughts and aligns her human mind to higher truth and creativity. Her human energy consciousness system is tuned to her divine core and she expresses herself as a cosmic light being. She incarnated as a blessing and now she can tune into the flow of all the blessings and light flowing through her.

Forgiveness Heals Generational Trauma

By broadening our perspective and understanding that transgenerational memories are recorded within the experiences of all humanity, we learn how to avoid becoming trapped in the blame game. Let's try not to hold onto resentment, unforgiveness, and despair based on the transgenerational negative love bonds we discover along the way. Yes, you were hurt, and it's important to acknowledge the pain, but after that you should strive to unravel a greater mystery and reclaim your divine heritage. You may need to go through stages of your healing process, but that is perfectly okay.

Identifying old resentments like anger, grief, and unforgiveness is key to revealing the negative love bond patterns, as it's the unresolved hurt and pain that keep you recycling those old transgenerational patterns. The first step of transformation occurs with this insight; then, when you lift your consciousness to illuminate the old patterns, forgiveness holds the key to the transfiguration process. Christ says to Peter, "Forgive seventy times seven" (*Holy Bible, New International Version*, 2013/1973, Matt 18:22). It may take time to unleash the power of your core to unravel this deeper pain, hatred, jealousy, grief, or resentment. You may have to explore your need to hold onto the memory before forgiving the other—perhaps starting with forgiving the self.

You have the power to unravel the greater mystery within and heal yourself, your family, and even your ancestors as well. Forgiveness is the key that unlocks the forces that hold you entangled with the past. Forgiveness goes much deeper than saying, "I forgive you," which seldom works unless you have done deeper work. Many of us have held onto unforgiveness for years, and this only clouds our system even more. Instead of clinging to "I'll never forgive you," it is much better to seek the Divine inside and ask for forgiveness: "Forgive me for I have hated you, separated from you, blamed you for over 30 years or so." It's in this genuine humble apology that you will free yourself.

It is not easy to forgive; sometimes it takes time and continuous introspection to see if you have let go of all the pain and hurt. Think about any situation where you have said, "I forgive you," only to discover later that you have continued to bring the same issue up. This happens because you haven't gone deep enough. Within you are the kernel of truth and your core essence, contracted by hate, resentment, and unforgiveness.

Learning the basic principles of forgiveness can act as a key to freeing ourselves from transgenerational, personal, familial, and relational negative love bonds. Many of us have learned the concept that it is better to forgive. Yet, for some, this is harder than it sounds. Perhaps the trauma was so severe that it is unfathomable to forgive the other. I have learned over time that unforgiveness can start with the self first. This may sound counterintuitive, yet when understood and practiced it can open the doorway to peace and healing.

To start the process of forgiveness, you can use the following steps. These will help you to start with internal healing and then move outward to forgive those who have hurt you:

1. Keep a journal and write about the painful memories in your heart.

2. Identify people you are unable to forgive—even God, if you are holding on to unforgiveness there.

3. In meditation, sense how unforgiveness has impacted your life, your feelings, and your thoughts.

4. Have a conversation with the infinite intelligence within you. Be honest and open in the conversation.

5. Ask and pray: "Forgive me for hating you so much, for holding this anger, resentment, and pain in my heart for over 20 or 50 years."

6. Recognize how you have held onto the anger, pain, and rage and the impact it has had—and is still having—on you. You can write these realizations down to clarify any distortion that is separating you from transfiguring years of pain and unforgiveness.

7. Pray to release the burden in your heart.

8. You may not be able to forgive the other person yet, but you can release the entanglement between you.

9. This process can eventually lead to a change toward freeing yourself from the burden in your heart.

Chapter 10:

Collective Awakening

You are a cosmic being who has infinite potential within you. Your core radiates with divine qualities that you can manifest to change the lives of the people around you—your family, friends, colleagues, and community. If you understand who you truly are and embrace it, you can change your life and live out your true purpose. Everyone has a place in the world and a part to play in bringing humanity to full awareness of their cosmic nature.

Let's look at some of the advantages of knowing your divine nature in different areas of your life. All of us are looking for solutions and ways to get through our professional careers and serve the higher purpose of our community and world. Within you lie the answers to some of the problems you have been facing.

The light within you comes from one power. It either flows freely or is contracted in separation. The key to real freedom is unlocking the core quality that is suppressed inside waiting to become free again, choosing grace, forgiveness, understanding, and love over everything else. You may find this easier than you imagined. Freeing yourself from the negative love bonds and allowing divine wisdom, love, and grace to flow from you is the ultimate divine plan.

Let's review how we can apply these principles to our personal life, family life, career, community, corporate responsibility, and, ultimately, the world. How can we as divine cosmic beings become instruments of divine peace and blessings upon the world?

Transformation in Your Personal Life

The first area that unlocking the divine genogram will affect is your personal life. Once you understand who you are, you will be able to respect the divinity within and express it fully. From here, confidence and self-love will emanate as you walk in the full knowledge of yourself. It's like Marcus Garvey once said (Salazar, 2018):

> Man in the full knowledge of himself is a superb and supreme creature of creation. When man becomes possessor of the knowledge of himself, he becomes master of his environment, the captain of his own ship, the director of his own destiny, the accomplisher of his own ends. (para 1)

In the full knowledge of your divinity and cosmic nature, you transmit and receive divine blessings and wisdom from all of your relationships.

The I AM mantras and meditations offer you the opportunity to transform, transcend, and transfigure your negative love bonds into positive core expressions and healing. You will awaken the light within and offer hope and reconciliation to your family, friends, and colleagues. Consider making these mantras a healthy daily routine. In the beginning it will seem strange, but as you practice shifting from one polarity to the next and finding the middle way or fulcrum in the center, your light, love, and passion will emerge naturally.

Transformation in Your Work & Business

Next, let's explore how these changes can impact your career and business. Your frame of reference has now shifted toward being in alignment with your divine qualities, and your center of focus has shifted from a physical base reality to a cosmic, infinite intelligent, and loving universe reality. How does this shift impact your career choices? Does it impact the way you visualize your work, your contribution to your business, the team you manage, or the team you work on? Can you imagine the divine genogram within your employees and coworkers, customers, and supply chain? Be curious about how you and others are part of an infinite intelligent web of creative possibilities.

If you are the CEO of a large company or own a business, do your energy and your unhealed family patterns impact the company in either a positive or negative way? Consider adopting some of the principles in this book to shift or change the energy and consciousness flow within your business. If you are an employee, how are you contributing to the highest function of your team or the wider organization? Let's review a few ways you can apply the principles in your workplace.

As a leader or employee, understanding the interconnectedness and cosmic nature of your existence starts with awareness. By recognizing the morphogenetic resonance between all aspects of your business—from employees, to supply chains, to customers, to the environment—your company will be in harmony with the community and world. When you're working in a corporation as part of a group or team, you are working with a collective family/business field. Whether you manage a large corporation or a small business, your resonance and transmission of divine qualities have a far-reaching impact. Imagine everyone you touch impacting another person, whereby the resonant field grows to their family, the community, and the world.

As previously mentioned, people interact based on how they match each other to somebody already within their family. For instance, some might see their colleagues as their older brothers or their younger sisters and so forth. In some cases, you can hear people in the work setting saying things like "You are like a brother to me" or "You are like a father to me"—which, recognize it or not, is often an additional correlation to the family members we already know. So, we might feel comfortable with or in competition with somebody based on who we map them to in our family systems.

You can enhance group cohesiveness by embodying these principles and emanating a cohesive field for the collective. It is the leader's biofield that co-regulates the company's cohesiveness and contribution to the world. According to Robert Anderson and William Adams (2019), thought leaders and authors of *Scaling Leadership* and creators of the *Leadership Circle 360 Profile*, the stewardship of a great leader allows them to navigate reactivity within the company and steer the employees into creativity. Reactivity can be a clue that some aspect of the business needs attention. It highlights an entanglement within the system that can lead to great change. A strong leader in a corporation understands how to modify their reactivity to understand and navigate their employees' reactivity. This ultimately scales the company into creative productivity in harmony with the world.

Discovering and acknowledging the gifts and challenges of all team members offers you the opportunity to inspire each member to grow in creativity, as well as encouraging collective productivity. Every employee has unique gifts as well as challenges to overcome. Finding the fulcrum in the center is where your light can transmit and engage others to reach their highest potential and ultimate joy in the workplace.

A tree's purpose is not only to survive the weather but to bear fruit and reproduce after its kind as well. It is great if you can transform your personal life by unlocking the divine genogram, but there is also an opportunity to bring blessings that can transform your business, work, or leadership skills.

Community & World Transformation

The divine qualities that emanate from our core transform our personal lives, our work, our communities, and ultimately the world at large. Accessing the light and blessings within everyone uplifts humanity and heals nations. The light that shines within us is a witness to the interconnectedness of everything alive. When we emanate divine wisdom, divine love, and divine will, we ultimately respect each other and build healthy communities and societies that thrive in a shared vision of the world.

Perhaps the world is a great cosmic experiment, where we are all connected via the infinite intelligent, loving universe regardless of our culture, race, gender, or caste in life. It is our unified light and blessings that help heal humanity and all sentient life on our beautiful planet Earth.

Our joy and purpose also arise when we embrace our shared humanity. Kindness becomes our common language, spoken in countless small acts that brighten our days. It is in the smile we share with a stranger, the supportive words we offer to a friend, or the hand we lend to those in need. When we recognize that every act of love contributes to a greater harmony, we become the change we wish to see in the world. Each simple gesture creates ripples reaching far beyond our immediate surroundings, reminding us that we are all part of something bigger.

With every thoughtful conversation, we are able to bridge the gaps that separate us. When we become authored by listening from the divine within, we hear and respond from a different level of our beingness. Listening becomes an essential part of this transformation, allowing us to not just hear but truly understand where others are coming from. People share their stories, revealing not only their joys but also their struggles. What may appear as different paths can often lead to the same destination—a place of understanding, compassion, and shared experiences.

Embark on Your Journey

You have come to the end of this book with new insights for the beginning of your journey. I hope everything we have discussed has helped you open your eyes and understand the great potential that is within you. In the words of the apostle Paul, "I too pray that the eyes of your heart may be enlightened in order that you may know the hope to which he has called you, the riches of his glorious inheritance in you" (Holy Bible, New International Edition, 2013/1973, Ephesians 1:18).

May the blessings that you bring to the world manifest in your everyday life and work, and in the world as well. Your incarnation was a miraculous transfiguration that allowed you to shine your light on humanity. Walking in the understanding of your true nature is a fulfilling journey that will make you an instrument of divine peace. By returning to your roots, by integrating science, spirituality, and psychology, you are reclaiming your divine origins as a cosmic being having a human experience. You are lifting the shroud of profound forgetting and remembering your true nature.

May you unravel your divine qualities and potential and be inspired to be a light unto this world. For more information, visit my website (donnaevansstrauss.com) for upcoming classes, meditations, genogram worksheets, and blogs that support your journey and the evolution of our planet.

Glossary

- **Aura:** The auric field is an ancient term describing the energy field that radiates from all sentient life. It includes plants, animals, and inanimate objects (which are imbued with the owner's field or surrounding area).

- **Brennan Healing Science:** A holistic healing modality developed by Barbara Brennan that focuses on the human energy field, utilizing techniques like high-sense perception (HSP) for diagnosis and healing.

- **Chakra:** Cones of energy that are connected via the vertical power current. They directly nourish the body from the core essence dimension and receive energy from the surrounding environment. This includes people, animals, all forms of nature, and universal consciousness.

- **Chakra System:** A framework from Indian spiritual traditions describing seven energy centers within the human body, each associated with different physical, emotional, and spiritual functions.

- **Conscious Universe:** A concept proposing that consciousness is not merely a human phenomenon but an intrinsic aspect of the cosmos.

- **Core Star:** The original divine spark, and the light given to all sentient life. It includes all the radiant divine qualities expressed by humanity and other sentient beings.

- **Dimensions:** Deeper levels of consciousness in time and space. Dimensions relate to each other in a holographic way and are inclusive of each other.

- **Divine Love:** The frequency of transfigurative love as it enters human consciousness and guides our spiritual growth.

- **Divine Quality:** A spiritual gift that is innate and universal in nature.

- **Energy Bodies:** Layers of the human energy field that correspond to different aspects of existence, including the etheric, emotional, mental, and causal bodies.

- **Energy Centers:** Points in the human body that facilitate the flow of life force energy (prana, qi), such as chakras and acupuncture points.

- **Extrasensory Perception (ESP):** A set of abilities allowing individuals to gain information beyond the known physical senses, including telepathy, clairvoyance, and precognition.

- **Fear Bands:** The expression of consciousness by all sentient life that emanates fear and surrounds a person or animal, a group of people or animals, and the Earth. It relates to terror and fight, flight, freeze, fawn, or flop responses in the deep limbic system and nervous system.

- **Four Dimensions of Human Kind:** There are four dimensions described in Barbara Brennan's book *Light Emerging*. These are the physical, human energy consciousness system (HECS), hara, and core star. Within each dimension, there is an expression for the core star dimension. The individuated core essence is part of the universal divine consciousness.

- **God:** Infinite intelligent universe, teeming with life, transfigurative love, and the divine design of visible and invisible.

- *Hands of Light*: A book by Barbara Brennan that explores energy healing and redefines ESP as high-sense perception (HSP).

- **Hara Dimension:** The dimension of intention that resides deeper than the chakras and seven levels of the human energy consciousness system (HECS). The individuated core essence intends to incarnate and has three points of individuation: the ID point above the head, the soul seat in the high heart, and the tan tien in the lower abdomen. The core essence upwells through this dimension, which becomes the access point for the HECS, which includes the vertical power current.

- **High-Sense Perception (HSP):** A term coined by Barbara Brennan to describe heightened intuitive and sensory abilities beyond the traditional five senses.

- **Holistic Perspective:** A viewpoint that considers the whole system rather than focusing on individual parts, emphasizing interconnectedness and interdependence.

- **Hologram:** A three-dimensional image reproduced from a pattern of interference produced by a split coherent beam of radiation (such as a laser).

- **Holographic Universe Theory:** A concept suggesting that every part of the universe contains information about the whole, akin to a hologram where each fragment mirrors the entire image.

- **Human Biofield:** The field of energy and information that surrounds and interpenetrates the human body, influencing health and well-being.

- **Human Energy Consciousness Field (HECS):** The interconnections of the seven chakras and seven levels of the human energy field related to physical, emotional, mental, relational, and spiritual aspects of consciousness. Barbara Brennan suggested that energy and consciousness cannot be separated.

- **Human Energy Consciousness System (HECS):** Barbara Brennan coined this term to describe the energy and consciousness that surrounds the body and permeates every cell. It includes seven major chakras and 21 minor chakras and vertical power currents that radiate into seven levels of consciousness. This consciousness reflects our psychological functions and nourishes each of our organs and body systems. The HECS arises out of the individuated core star and hara dimensions.

- **Human Love:** The frequency of love changes as it enters into human relationships. It can appear in a kaleidoscope of ways, and can be subdued or radiated based on human life experiences and our sense of belonging and acceptance.

- **Infinite Intelligent Universe:** The invisible cosmic intelligence field that informs the universe. The universe is seen as a hologram where within each part is the whole.

- **Metaphysical:** Concerned with the nature of reality beyond the physical, often involving philosophical and spiritual inquiry.

- **Negative Intentionality:** The divine qualities when expressed change due to defenses in the human energy consciousness system. Examples would be love becoming bonded with criticism, or trust becoming mistrust and bonded with fear.

- **Negative Love Bond:** When love becomes frozen in time and bonded with a painful life experience and thoughts. This can be transmitted generationally as unhealthy habits and life experiences.

- **Noise Bands:** Human consciousness bands around the Earth that include all productivity that creates waves of sound and frequencies.

- **Nonlocality:** A concept in quantum physics where particles separated by vast distances can instantaneously affect each other's states, potentially analogous to interconnectedness in ESP.

- **Positive Intentionality:** The ability to direct your consciousness (divine qualities such as love) from the core in a positive way that impacts the life force emanating from the chakra system and vertical power current into the human energy consciousness field.

- **Positive Love Bond:** When love is expressed from the core and is bonded in a healthy way with other human beings or sentient life.

- **Quantum Biology:** The study of quantum phenomena in

biological systems, exploring how quantum principles may influence biological processes such as brain function and consciousness.

- **Quantum Mechanics:** A fundamental theory in physics describing the behavior of energy and matter at the smallest scales, often referenced in discussions about the nature of consciousness and ESP.

- **Quantum Physics:** The branch of physics that deals with the behavior of particles at the smallest scales, often challenging traditional Newtonian physics with concepts like wave–particle duality and entanglement.

- **Rainbow Bridge:** The windows of grace, seals, or portals within the chakras and vertical power current on the fluid levels of the field act as a bridge to the human energy consciousness field and to the hara dimension. Each level refracts and reflects color emerging from the core light into the physical world.

- **Seals of Chakras:** A concept introduced by Barbara Brennan. Seals are located as windows or access points between each chakra and each of the seven levels of the human energy consciousness system.

- **Self-Love:** The frequency of love changes again. When clear and transparent, it relates to our experience of self-love and self-acceptance regardless of our faults. It can be suppressed by developmental trauma and unresolved emotional conflicts.

- **Synchronicity:** A concept introduced by Carl Jung referring to the meaningful coincidence of events that appear to be causally unrelated but are experienced as occurring together in a significant manner.

- **The Cosmic Hologram:** A book by Jude Currivan proposing that the universe operates as a hologram, with information serving as its foundational element.

- **Transfigurative Love:** Indescribable transformative power of love as an innate gift, considered by many wisdom teachers as the connective invisible tissue of the universe. There is only one love in the universe. We do not make more love but rather surrender into the different frequencies as it subscends into human consciousness. The frequency changes at each level of the human energy consciousness field.

- **Universal Field:** A theoretical concept proposing that all information and energy in the universe are interconnected, allowing for phenomena like ESP.

- **Vertical Power Current:** Part of the human energy consciousness system that connects the chakras and transmits energy from the core and hara dimensions into the human energy consciousness field and physical body. It is like an energetic highway that connects each of the dimensions, and is the informational transporting system that creates the foundation for the physical body.

- **Windows of Grace:** The seals of chakras become the windows of grace as each of the seven major divine qualities is transmitted from the core dimension, through the hara dimension, through the chakra seals, and into the human energy consciousness system.

References

Amen, D. G. (2016). Change your brain, change your life. Piatkus. (Original work published 1998)

Anderson, R. J., & Adams, W. A. (2019). Scaling leadership : Building organizational capability and capacity to create outcomes that matter most. John Wiley & Sons, Inc.

Baksa, P. B. (2011, October 3). The zero point field: How thoughts become matter? HuffPost. https://www.huffpost.com/entry/zero-point-field_b_913831

Big Think. (2014, February 24). Michio Kaku: This is your brain on a laser beam: Big Think [Video]. YouTube. https://www.youtube.com/watch?v=aUUl3YPDcAE

Bite-sized Philosophy. (2017, December 12). Jordan Peterson - is your pain real? [Video]. YouTube. https://www.youtube.com/watch?v=cAdqytOHSE0

Brennan, B. A. (2011a). *Hands of light*: A guide to healing through the human energy field. Bantam.

Brennan, B. A. (2011b). *Light emerging: The journey of personal healing*. Bantam.

Brennan, B. A. (1999 - 2009). *Seeds of the spitit*. Barbara Brennan Inc.

Brennan, B. A. (2017). *Core light healing: My personal journey and advanced healing concepts for creating the life you long to live*. Hay House.

Brennan healing sessions. (n.d.). Vera de Chalambert. https://www.veradechalambert.com/barbarabrennan

Centre for Addiction and Mental Health. (n.d.). Trauma. https://www.camh.ca/en/health-info/mental-illness-and-addiction-index/trauma

Chabris, C., & Simons, D. (2011). The invisible gorilla: And other ways our intuitions deceive us. Harmony.

Childs Heyl, J. (2024, January 16). The Flynn effect: What's behind rising IQ scores? Verywell Mind. https://www.verywellmind.com/the-flynn-effect-7565614

Colón-Ramos lab. (n.d.). Yale School of Medicine. https://medicine.yale.edu/lab/colon_ramos/overview/

Currivan, J. (2017). The cosmic hologram. Simon and Schuster.

Descartes, R. (2008). Discourse on the method and the meditation (J. Veitch, Trans.). Cosimo Classics. (Original work published 1637)

Divisions of the autonomic nervous system. (n.d.). Lumen Learning. https://courses.lumenlearning.com/suny-ap1/chapter/divisions-of-the-autonomic-nervous-system/

Strauss, D. E. (2025). The cosmic breath. Donna Evans Strauss.

Einstein, A., Podolsky, B., & Rosen, N. (1935). Can quantum-mechanical description of physical reality be considered complete? Physical Review, 47(10), 777–780. https://doi.org/10.1103/physrev.47.777

Forbes, N., & Mahon, B. (2014). Faraday, Maxwell, and the electromagnetic field: How two men revolutionized physics. Prometheus Books.

Freud, S., & Hall, G. S. (2018). A general introduction to psychoanalysis: A history of psychoanalytic theory, treatment and therapy. Adansonia Press.

Graves, K. (1875). *The world's sixteen crucified saviors*. Freethought Press.

Greatness Coaching. (2018, January 17). Bruce Lipton explains epigenetics [Video]. YouTube. https://www.youtube.com/watch?v=VNvEAkZSBEU

Groen, G. J., Baljet, B., & Drukker, J. (1990). Nerves and nerve plexuses of the human vertebral column. American Journal of Anatomy, 188(3), 282–296. https://doi.org/10.1002/aja.1001880307

Hawking, S. W. (1974). Black hole explosions? Nature, 248(5443), 30–31. https://doi.org/10.1038/248030a0

Holy Bible, New International Version. (2013). Zondervan. (Original work published 1973)

Hooft, G. (1993). Dimensional reduction in quantum gravity. Conf. Proc. C, 930308, 284–296.

Jablonka, E., & Lamb, M. J. (1999). *Epigenetic inheritance and evolution: The Lamarckian dimension.* Oxford University Press.

Kaku, M. (2022). *The God equation*: The quest for a theory of everything. Anchor.

Karma-glin-pa. (2017). The Tibetan book of the dead (J. Baldock, Ed., & Zla-ba-bsam-'grub, Trans.). Sirius.

Kulbatski, I. (2023, August 4). Shaping brain recovery using bioelectricity. The Scientist. https://www.the-scientist.com/shaping-brain-recovery-using-bioelectricity-71252

László, E. (2007). Science and the Akashic field. Simon and Schuster.

Leadership circle profile. (n.d.). The Leadership Circle. https://leadershipcircle.com/leadership-assessment-tools/leadership-circle-profile/

Lemaître, G., Stoffel, J.-F., & Govaerts, J. (2019). Learning the physics of Einstein with Georges Lemaître: Before the big bang theory. Springer.

Lipton, B. H. (2005). The biology of belief: Unleashing the power of consciousness, matter & miracles. Mountain of Love/Elite Books.

Lipton, B. H., & Bhaerman, S. (2011). Spontaneous evolution: Our positive future (and a way to get there from here). Hay House.

Lowenstein, D. H., Thomas, M. J., Smith, D. H., & McIntosh, T. K. (1992). Selective vulnerability of dentate hilar neurons following traumatic brain injury: A potential mechanistic link between head trauma and disorders of the hippocampus. Journal of Neuroscience, 12(12), 4846–4853. https://doi.org/10.1523/jneurosci.12-12-04846.1992

Luchte, J. (2009). Pythagoras and the doctrine of transmigration: Wandering souls. Continuum.

MacQueen, H. (2023, August 1). Sperm counts. The Open University. https://www.open.edu/openlearn/nature-environment/natural-history/sperm-counts

Maestripieri, D. (2012, March 20). What monkeys can teach us about human behavior: From facts to fiction. Psychology Today. https://www.psychologytoday.com/us/blog/games-primates-play/201203/what-monkeys-can-teach-us-about-human-behavior-facts-fiction

Maharishi Mahesh Yogi. (1967). Maharishi Mahesh Yogi on the Bhagavad-Gita. Penguin Books.

Maldacena, J. (1998). The large N limit of superconformal field theories and supergravity. Advances in Theoretical and Mathematical Physics, 2(2), 231–252. https://doi.org/10.4310/atmp.1998.v2.n2.a1

Mangalam Research Centre. (2024, May 16). Jim Tucker, "Children who remember previous lives" [Video]. Vimeo. https://vimeo.com/946809244/ada878f19e?share=copy

Manné, J. (2009). Family constellations: A practical guide to uncovering the origins of family conflict. North Atlantic Books.

Matchar, E. (2017, May 26). Tweaking the tiny electrical charges inside cells can fight infection. Smithsonian Magazine.

https://www.smithsonianmag.com/innovation/using-bodys-own-electricity-fight-infection-180963460/

McLeod, S. (2024, January 24). Carl Jung's theory of personality: Archetypes & collective unconscious. Simply Psychology. https://www.simplypsychology.org/carl-jung.html

Minuchin, S. (1974). Families & family therapy. Harvard University Press.

Moreno, J. L. (1964). Psychodrama (3rd edition). Psychodrama Press.

Moskowitz, C. (2014, August 5). Fact or fiction?: Energy can neither be created nor destroyed. Scientific American. https://www.scientificamerican.com/article/energy-can-neither-be-created-nor-destroyed/

Newberg, A. B., & Waldman, M. R. (2010). *How God changes your brain: Breakthrough findings from a leading neuroscientist.* Ballantine Books.

Paul, C. (2022, April 29). Nikola Tesla told him: "Bury your findings until humanity is ready." Messy Nessy. https://www.messynessychic.com/2022/04/27/nikola-tesla-told-him-bury-your-findings-until-humanity-is-ready/

Penzias, A. A. (1968). Measurement of cosmic microwave background radiation. IEEE Transactions on Microwave Theory and Techniques, 16(9), 608–611. https://doi.org/10.1109/tmtt.1968.1126760

Pert, C. B. (2003). *Molecules of emotion: The science behind mind–body medicine.* Scribner.

Pythagoras. (n.d.). Pythagoras quote. A-Z Quotes. https://www.azquotes.com/quote/1138548

Rastogi, R., Saxena, M., Gupta, M., Kohli, V., Kumar, P., & Jain, M. (2021). Visualizations of human bioelectricity with internal symptom captures: The Indo-Vedic concepts on Healthcare 4.0. In Jain, V., Chatterjee, J. M., Hedayati, H., Krit, S.,

& Deperlioglu, O. (Eds.), Deep learning for personalized healthcare services (pp. 67–90). De Gruyter.

Russell, W. (1947). The secret of light. Рипол Классик.

Russell, W., & Russell, L. (1926). *The universal one.* An exact science of the one visible and invisible universe of mind. Brieger Press.

Salazar, R. (2018, October 4). Man in the full knowledge of himself is a superb and supreme creature of creation. Medium. https://medium.com/@osnerenso/man-in-the-full-knowledge-of-himself-is-a-superb-and-supreme-creature-of-creation-ede681ac2ce1

Sanskrit. (n.d.). Lumen Learning. https://courses.lumenlearning.com/suny-hccc-worldcivilization/chapter/sanskrit/

Sheldrake, R. (1995). A new science of life: The hypothesis of morphic resonance. Park Street Press.

Sheldrake, R. (2009). Morphic resonance: The nature of formative causation. Park Street Press.

Sheldrake, R. (2011). *Dogs that know when their owners are coming home: And other unexplained powers of animals.* Three Rivers Press.

Shvat, A. (2016, August 21). Why is Elohim in the plural. Yeshiva. https://www.yeshiva.co/ask/58976

6 mythical dragons from different cultures. (n.d.). Dragons and Mythical Beasts. https://www.dragonsandbeastslive.com/blog/6-mythical-dragons-from-different-cultures

Susskind, L. (1995). The world as a hologram. Journal of Mathematical Physics, 36(11), 6377–6396. https://doi.org/10.1063/1.531249

Trahan, L. H., Stuebing, K. K., Fletcher, J. M., & Hiscock, M. (2014). The Flynn effect: a meta-analysis. Psychological Bulletin, 140(5), 1332–1360. https://doi.org/10.1037/

Tucker, J. B. (2016). The case of James Leininger: An American case of the reincarnation type. Explore, 12(3), 200–207. https://doi.org/10.1016/j.explore.2016.02.003

Turner, B. (2023, August 24). Quantum 'yin-yang' shows two photons being entangled in real-time. Live Science. https://www.livescience.com/physics-mathematics/quantum-physics/quantum-yin-yang-shows-two-photons-being-entangled-in-real-time

Van der Kolk, B. (2014). The body keeps the score: Brain, mind, and body in the healing of trauma. Penguin Books.

Whitfield, C. L. (2004). The truth about mental illness: Choices for healing. HCI.

Xie, P., Wu, K., Zheng, Y., Guo, Y., Yang, Y., He, J., Ding, Y., & Peng, H. (2018). Prevalence of childhood trauma and correlations between childhood trauma, suicidal ideation, and social support in patients with depression, bipolar disorder, and schizophrenia in southern China. Journal of Affective Disorders, 228, 41–48. https://doi.org/10.1016/j.jad.2017.11.011

Yehuda, R., & Lehrner, A. (2018). Intergenerational transmission of trauma effects: Putative role of epigenetic mechanisms. World Psychiatry, 17(3), 243–257. https://doi.org/10.1002/wps.20568

Other titles by Donna Evans Strauss

Find more resources to help you unleash the divine potential within.

www.donnaevansstrauss.com

www.ingramcontent.com/pod-product-compliance
Lightning Source LLC
Chambersburg PA
CBHW061734070526
44585CB00024B/2666